MArch UD

Urban Design
2012-2013

**The Bartlett
School of Architecture
UCL**

B pro

Bartlett Prospective

B-Pro

B-Pro, Bartlett Prospective, is a new global postgraduate entity within the School of Architecture currently composed of two courses: MArch Graduate Architectural Design (GAD), an advanced programme led by Alisa Andrasek (Biothing), providing access to the most sophisticated research in design and fabrication; and MArch Urban Design (UD), led by Adrian Lahoud, an advanced programme open to critical and theoretical strategies in urbanism and offering new approaches to planning cities.

The one-year B-Pro programmes are open to a diverse international student cohort and offer highly structured access to the realisation and application of research, and to the production of new schemes of conception and construction in architecture and urbanism. Housed in the School's newly acquired Royal Ear Hospital building, B-Pro has developed numerous lectures, seminars and workshops to underpin these ideas and promote a broad dialogue.

To this end, the 2012-2013 MArch GAD course was organised around eight Research Clusters driven by their respective tutors. These Clusters featured specific research in a number of domains, and offered the opportunity to gain access to new computational tools and a new culture of scripting, directly connected to tools of fabrication. Inspired by, and directly related to, the current scene of international architecture creation, the teaching of software packages such as Maya, Grasshopper, Arduino, Processing and other generative platforms comes from the perspective of an innovative idea of conception and fabrication in association with new digital production facilities (robots, SLS printing, advanced CNC tools etc).

Based on a global overview of the Mediterranean context, the 2012-2013 MArch UD course offered new theoretical schemes to analyse this complex social, cultural, economical and political territory, each of the seven Clusters of the MArch UD working on a specific city (Algiers, Athens, Beirut, Marseille, Messina & Reggio Calabria, Tangier, Tunis). Alternative proposals based on new morphological concepts and protocols were developed in response to urban field studies.

The Bartlett International Lecture Series – with numerous speakers, architects, historians and theoreticians – presented the opportunity for students to be confronted by the main streams of research that will be influential in the near future. Students' work evolved through different crit sessions and the final exhibition in the Royal Ear Hospital, with the presentation of drawings, models and animations, all of a very high quality, which clearly demonstrate the intense activity undertaken throughout the year.

Through the federative idea of creative architecture, B-Pro is an opportunity for students to find a way to participate in a new community and to affirm the singularity and originality of individual talents. These programmes are not only an open door to advanced architecture but also the base from which each student can define a singular practice and invent a strategy to find a position in the professional world.

From 2013, B-Pro will incorporate the MA in the History and Theory of Architecture, to create a larger field of research in theory and to stimulate new exchanges between the three poles of the programme. The school's production facilities will be enhanced with B-Made, a global entity for fabrication which launched in 2013, and the opening of a real factory space.

The 2013 B-Pro exhibition and the publication of this book provide an excellent overview of the depth of quality and the intensity of the teaching of The Bartlett's tutors. What they also showcase is the passion of all the students involved.

Frédéric Migayrou
Bartlett Professor of Architecture
Director of B-Pro

MArch Urban Design
Forms of Life

Urban design works on three kinds of things. The first is *relations,* those between people, and with the world. Forms of association, belonging, collectivity and interaction bind human beings through common activities, beliefs or shared perceptions. Work, social ties, kinship and institutions express the modes of natural sociality characteristic to human beings. The second type of thing that urban design works with is *protocols*, the various laws, codes, norms and conventions that organise, limit and finally secure certain kinds of human behaviour. *Protocols* distinguish between the acceptable and the prohibited, orienting life towards specific ends. The third thing is *repetition*, which concerns the machinic reproduction of routines, habits and other typical behaviours – the rhythms of everyday life, their points of attraction and repulsion – whether to consume or to compete, to cultivate the self or entrain one's life to cycles of work and respite.

Because these various materials are always already in play, there is no *tabula rasa*. In urban design each project enters – not into a vacuum – but an already existing diagram of contradictory tensions and conflicts. This is not to say that the above is simply given, on the contrary we have the freedom and responsibility to claim new forms of sociality or work, to enter into different kinds of common agreement, propose alternative conventions or protocols – that is to say, we reserve the right to compose our collective form of life in other ways. Urban design turns space into an instrument in an attempt to affect these kinds of transformations. In order for space to be instrumentalised effectively, it cannot ignore these constraints, rather it must work through them, forming a praxis whose reach extends beyond the academy into the city where the dispute over spatial coexistence reaches a singular intensity.

In this, the first year of the refreshed MArch Urban Design programme, the strongest projects succeeded in marshalling a set of spatial principles that work *through* and *on* these things. Moreover, they do so across multiple scales, binding near and far, weak and strong, small and large. All this must materialise in the specificity of the form proposed and its relation to the context – that is to say, in design. Beyond their comprehensiveness as research proposals lies the intelligence to identify an entry point to the force-field, a specific moment of sensitivity whose transformation might cascade beyond the limits of the intervention. As Benjamin writes to Bloch 'Everything will be as it is now, just a little different'. This small difference – no matter how imperceptible and recalcitrant to transformation it might be – finally changes everything.

Adrian Lahoud
Programme Leader

MArch Urban Design is a 12-month full-time post-professional course that sets out to transform existing paradigms of urban design education, aiming to open inquiry into social, anthropological, economic and ecological concerns in a context where the political and ethical responsibility of the designer is seen as fundamental. A sustained and comprehensive engagement with the realities of urbanisation is cultivated through extensive research and fieldwork, providing a rigorous platform for design experimentation. The programme is structured into seven Research Clusters, bringing together a new generation of designers and thinkers from across the world in order to provide rich and challenging spaces for long-term research on urbanisation and design. Every three years a single geopolitical region will act as a common object of inquiry for the entire programme.

Contents

Tangier: Elia Zenghelis second workshop crit preparation

Urban Design workshop reviews in the studio
with Platon Issaias and Adrian Lahoud

Messina Crits: students in discussion with the tutors, Davide Sacconi and Luca Galofaro

Tangier: Elia Zenghelis' workshop

Messina field trip: abandoned fort along Reggio Calabria's coastline

Athens field trip: students and tutors on the top of the Acropolis, with the urban landscape of Athens spilling off beyond the horizon

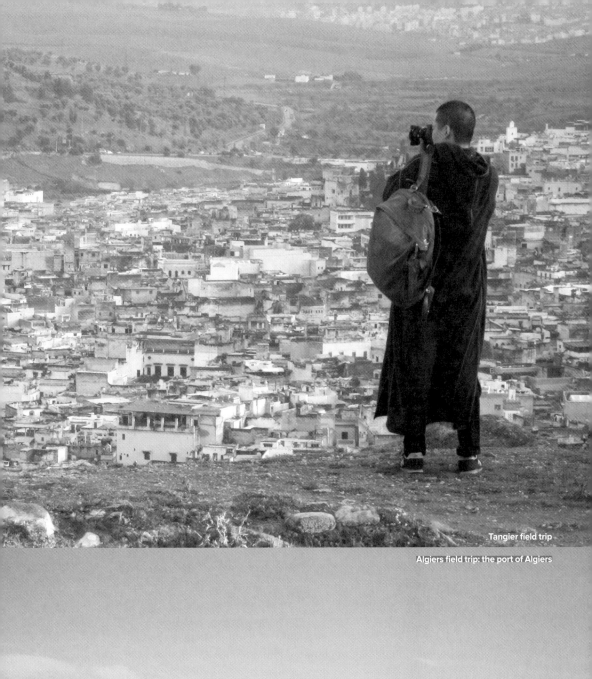

Tangier field trip

Algiers field trip: the port of Algiers

Algiers

1

Precipice of Change:
A New DNA for the City

Beth Hughes, DaeWha Kang

Once a fabled pirating town lording control over the Mediterranean, a strategic stronghold of the French colonial empire, and capital of the largest African nation, Algiers is now crumbling in decay, groaning under the burden of its inefficient and ill-conceived expansion. Recognising the inadequacy of its infrastructure and the great inequality manifested in its urban fabric, the government has mustered the political will and ambition to address its problems and restore itself to former glory. Unsullied by the tourism and irreverent development that have overtaken the rest of the Maghreb, Algiers is on a precipice.

We see the Gulf recipe, popularised by Dubai and exported to the rest of the world, as symptomatic of an urban calculus gone awry: focussed on speculative profits today and leading to catastrophic failure tomorrow. The architectural language of these financial speculations is driven more by an international iconography of luxury than thoughtful reflection on context; towers of glass and aluminium are dropped like dream palaces into scorching sandy deserts and freezing tundra without concern for local conditions. As this model sweeps through the world, rapidly expanding economies begin to yearn for the same shining economic model of urban growth. Already tempted by the Gulf recipe with its promises for economic success and instant urban restoration, Algiers is flirting with some dangerous images for the future.

Urban design is at a turning point where we must challenge our fundamental value systems and our existing development models. Somewhere along the line we have allowed a complex, messy, and rich urban calculus to be replaced by a derivative, reductive political and economic recipe: a recipe that sacrifices a sustainable future for the mirage of speculative profits today. The question for Algiers, before it is too late, is whether an alternative model exists: a model able to deliver economic performance whilst responding to the failings of the past. We must redefine the terms of our engagement to find alternatives measures of value; in Algiers we have found the perfect site for these investigations.

With the rapid growth and urbanisation of the world it is increasingly difficult to instigate real and widespread change within the traditional domains of the urban designer. The studio pursues the idea that true radical change will only be achieved through manipulation of the structures and systems that motivate development models, rather than focussing on the forms that these developments take.

The solution is not to propose yet another stylistic makeover or aesthetic language. We need to re-programme the very basis of development. New typologies, as the building blocks of development, can contain within themselves the possibility for the new value systems we propose. Providing a credible alternative to existing models requires developing design methodologies that can be measured according to an alternative calculus. We focus on identifying the factors that promise value beyond economic wealth and success, broadening and redefining our understanding of the term 'value' to include factors such as equality, religious and political freedom, social cohesion, energy and resource efficiency, access to transport, quality public space, and education within the urban realm.

By focussing on the creation of new typologies, we create systems rather than individual design interventions, and by focussing on the mechanisms of development, we can operate even in cities like Algiers where central planning and control has historically been unsuccessful. Through a combination of computational tools and traditional methods, we can test the many possible outcomes of this re-programming of the urban DNA, and move towards a more measurable, calculable vision for the future of our cities.

We would like to thank the tutors in the studio who have offered ongoing feedback to the Cluster over the course of the year. We'd like thank our guest tutors and critics: Naiara Vegara, Brian Dale, Jane Rendell, Jonathan Hill, Matthew Butcher, Godofredo Pereira, Christopher Choa, Tarsha Finney, and Hussam Chakouf, and Elia Zhengelis. Thank you also to our hosts during our Morocco field trip: Omar Allaoui, Bernard Ghesquierre, Samia Henni and Jean Paul Ichter.

Students
Fatema Al-Sehlawi, Lilin Chen, Yi-Ru Chen, Dimitra Christodoulou, Odysseas Diakakis, Di Feng, Georgios Garofalakis, Zheye Li, Katarzyna Plis, Stefanie Sebald, Tong Shen, Jie Yu, Meihui Yin

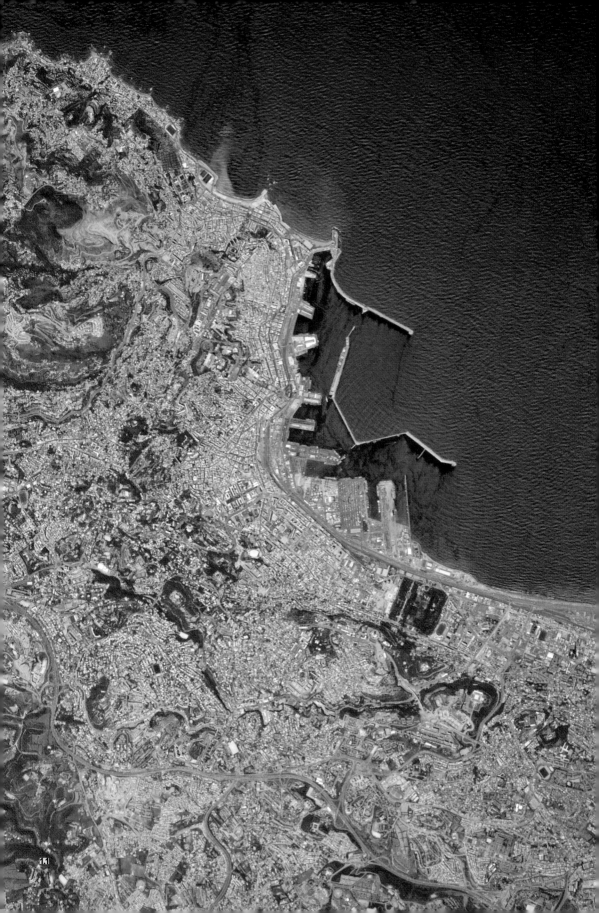

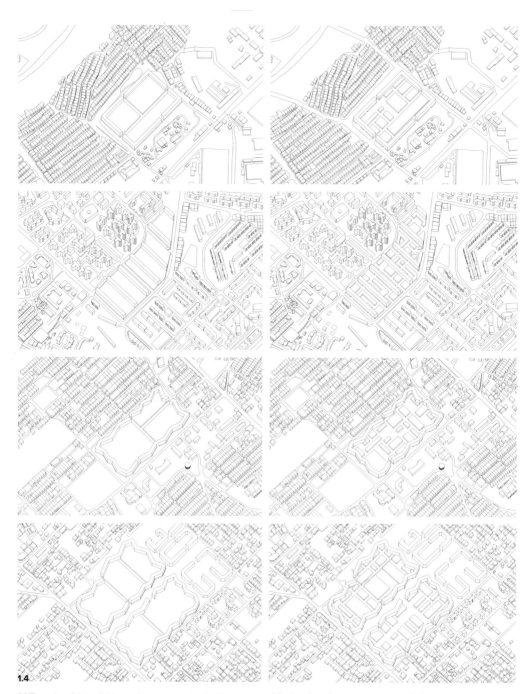

1.4

1.1 The urban fabric of Algiers showing a multitude of typologies. **1.2** Casbah and French Quarter Today. Photograph: François Prost. **1.3** New suburban tower developments. Photograph: Odysseas Diakakis. **1.4 – 1.11 Zheye Li, Meihui Yin, Tong Shen** In order to maintain the economic growth of Algiers during the global recession whilst simultaneously relieving local problems such as youth unemployment, housing shortage, urban separation combined with underutilised land and urban sprawl, the proposal sets up an economic model that promotes a cycle of consumption that operates as a form of acupuncture therapy for the city. This model is based on the understanding that all the majority of land ownership and development is handled by the state. The strategy is formulated as follows. 1. Create job opportunities for lower skilled workers through investment. 2. Gather large populations in a limited space. 3. Keep economic growth with basic consumption through high-density population. 4. Supply education resources to the larger population. 5. Replace with advanced consumption as a consequence of economic growth. 6. Replace with higher skilled jobs as a consequence of education. 7. Spread this model. **1.4** Implementation of the strategy according to plot conditions. **1.5** Plot permutations. **1.6** Phased plot development using the proposed economic model. **1.7 – 1.8** Phase 1 of strategy **1.9 – 1.10** Phase 2 of strategy. **1.11** Model of proposed strategy.

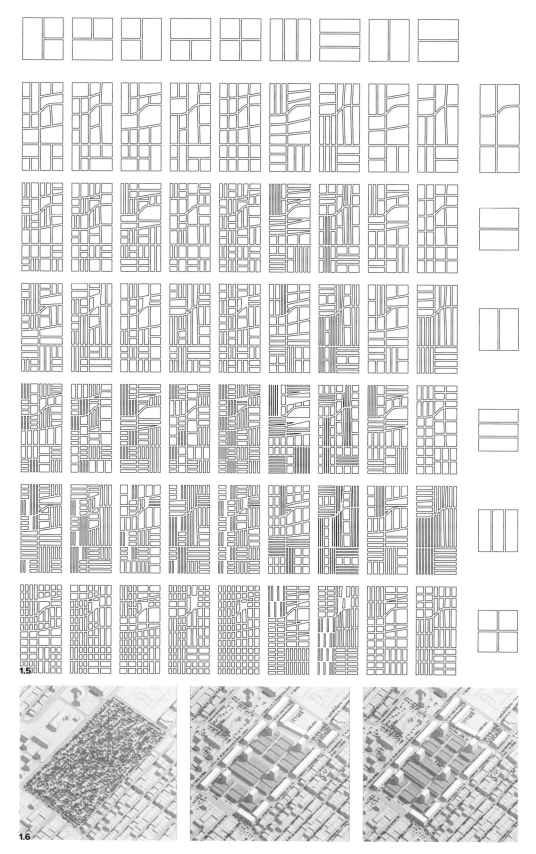

1.5

1.6

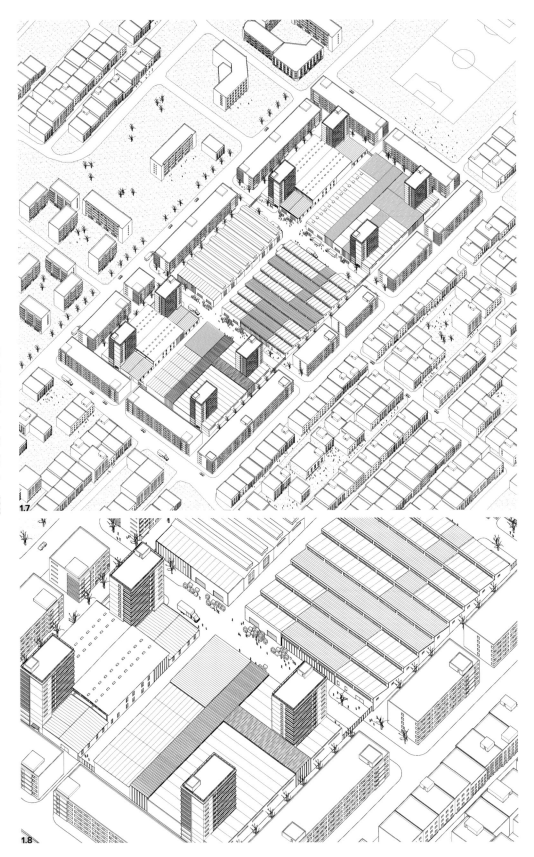

1.7

1.8

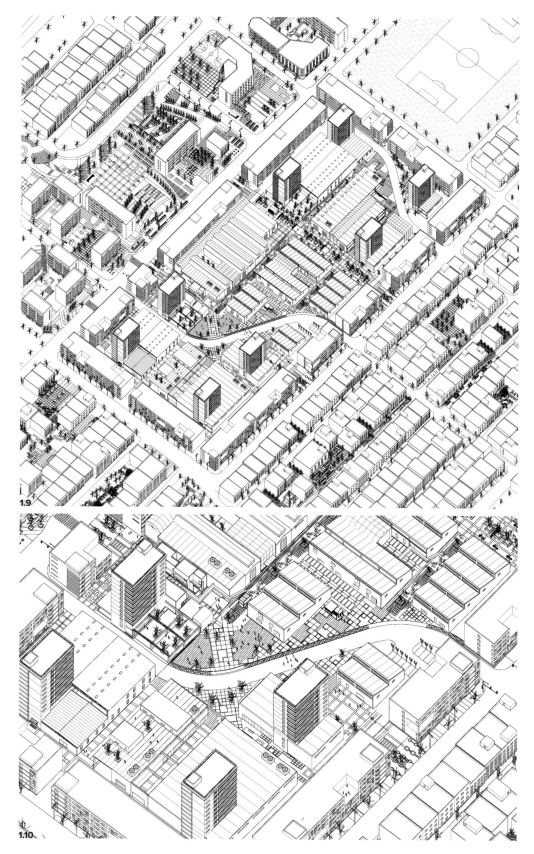

1.9

1.10

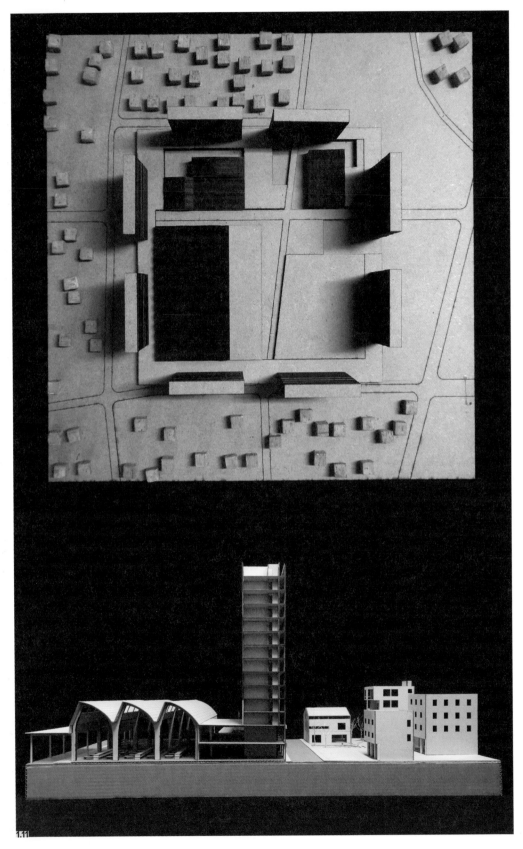

1.11

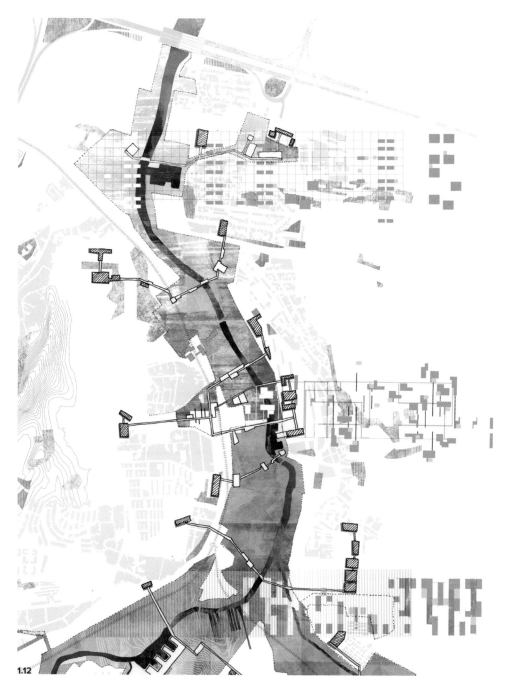

1.12

1.12 Georgios Garofalakis, Dimitra Christodoulou, Fatema Al-Sahlawi Strategy Plan for El-Harrach River, Algiers. The conceptual approach for the project is to identify the three distinct characters of the region: industrial, civic and agricultural. The river operates a spine supporting these characters which are then reinforced and promoted in order to stimulate the local economy and upgrade the urban environment. **1.13 – 1.18 Georgios Garofalakis, Dimitra Christodoulou, Fatema Al-Sahlawi** New Typologies. A series of typologies are generated to create a set of tools for mediating between social and spatial gaps present in the region of El Harrach. The proposed typologies respond to the various problems that have been identified within the context of Algiers: critical housing shortage, the monotonous housing

developments and the lack of a well developed urban environment. **1.14** Cluster. The different typologies are assembled together in varying configurations to create different common areas and gradients of public and private space. **1.15** Perspectives of the Civic Cluster, the Industrial Cluster and the Agricultural Cluster. **1.16** Sectional perspectives of the three Clusters.

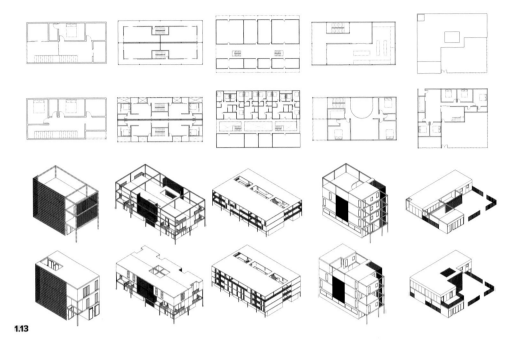

1.13

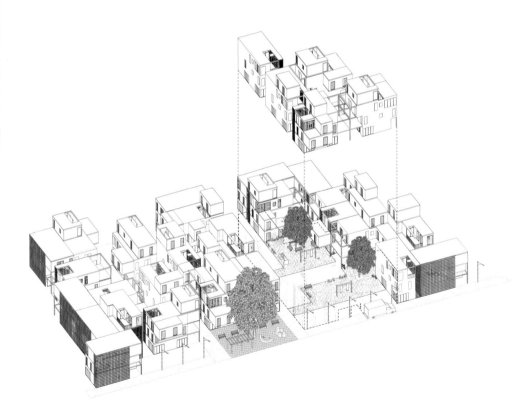

1.14

1.15

Civic quarter

Industrial quarter

1.16

Agricultural quarter

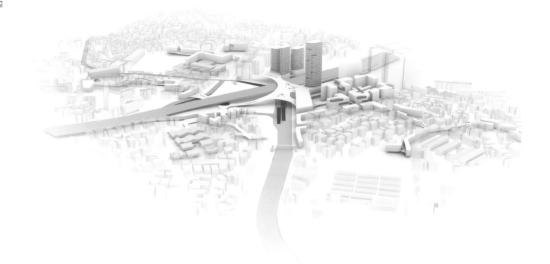

1.17

1.18

1.17 Di Feng, Lilin Chen Polycentrism – Algiers Secondary Centres, Overall Perspective. Following independence from France in 1962, Algiers has expanded dramatically whilst the Casbah and the French Colonial city remain at the centre playing a significant role in Algerian political, economic and regional development. Continual pressure from rural and international migration has resulted in the accumulation of bidonvilles, massive urban sprawl and the extension of urban life to the periphery of the city without the infrastructure to support it. The project aims to address these issues with the implementation of a series of secondary centres that attract new infrastructure and focus on transport hubs to create a new polycentric Algiers. **1.18 Di Feng, Lilin Chen** Polycentrism – Algiers Secondary Centre, Masterplan. The new centres are

implemented with the following strategy: 1. The new centres are located on transport interchanges with metro and bus stations under construction to capitalise on the new efficient transport hub. 2. Urban activity is extended in the new secondary centre by using the existing public buildings and spaces, such as mosques, schools, markets and playgrounds. 3. These public buildings and spaces are linked by a pedestrian network. This network also responds to local youth unemployment and housing shortage problems, encouraging interaction between the varying communities. 4. With the implementation of the linkages between existing community facilities and the new network the new secondary centre is able to be built up creating new areas of mixed use density.

1.19

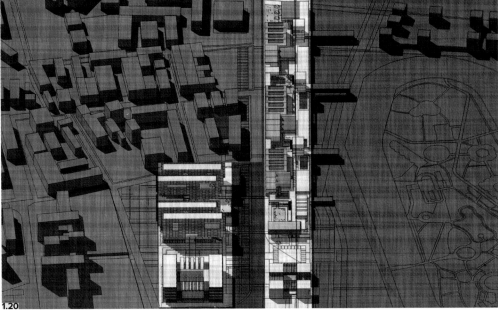

1.20

1.19 Jie Yu Plan of New Innovation Centre, Algiers. The project is envisioned as a new entrepreneurial incubation centre for small to medium-scale operators focussed on professional training. Its location is based on the government scheme for a new polycentric model adjacent to resources such as university, industry and business. The aim is to create a territory of innovation, a knowledge centre that builds up cooperation within the local context in order to maximise local potential and create opportunity for business development in response to youth unemployment and the transition of Algiers into the free market. Existing industrial buildings to the north of the site are used as the catalyst to establish a creative industry centre such as workshops and studio based start-up firms by renovating the existing industrial buildings.

1.20 Jie Yu Spatial Organisation. The new territory is not only in need of well defined spaces for small and medium scale businesses and research, but also more informal spaces for social encounters. This type of interaction has a vital impact on scientific research and creative thinking encouraging the small businesses to grow. The communal spaces are organised to influence and support the exchange of knowledge. The public spaces are organised within a hierarchy around two main axes bringing together the distinctive areas of the development in turn facilitating collaboration between the various groups.

1.21

1.22

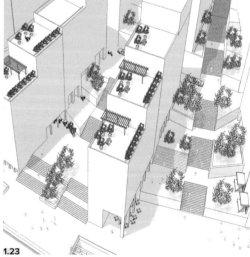

1.23

1.21 – 1.23 Stefanie Sebald Conceived as part of a city-wide strategy for intensification of urban areas around the existing centre, this proposal aims to complement the current masterplan of Algiers. A 25km transport loop expands the existing small public transport network to create a cohesive system in the topogrphically challenging areas around the centre connecting existing and new neighbourhoods to the city and to each other. Peculiar convex and concave conditions along the proposed tram, cycle and pedestrian path are created due to the steep terrain. The path is occupied by a series of building types developed to suit both the steep slopes as well as the spatial conditions created by the new curvlinear path creating new neighbourhoods. **1.21** Masterplan perspective showing manipulation of typologies according to topography. **1.22** Ridge plaza. **1.23** Convex condition.

1.24 Yi-Ru Chen The New Mediterranean Capital – Algiers Cruise Terminal Plan. Algiers is striving to become a part of the network of significant Mediterranean cities. The project imagines a scenario for the future whereby Algiers becomes a new Mediterranean Capital as part of the emerging potential of Maghreb countries. The port site creates an opportunity to deploy the idea of public space as a means of connection. The project turns the port towards the Mediterranean as well as back to the city centre as a form of public space. Bringing Algiers and the Mediterranean closer together, the project creates an overlap of these territories across the site.

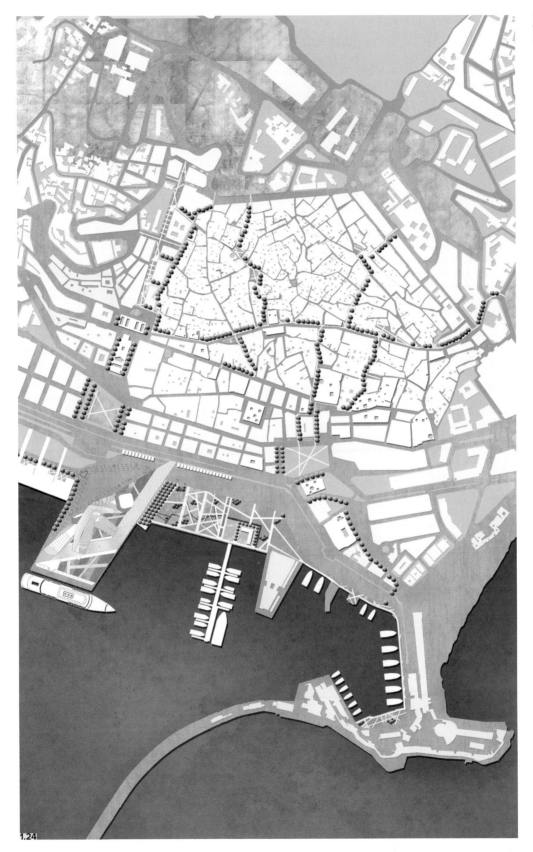

1.24

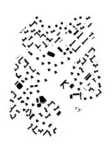

1.25

1.26

1.27

1.25 – 1.28 Odysseas Diakakis The project proposes a new hierarchy and mixed uses to replace the existing vast open spaces. The operation starts with a hypothetical solid fill from which the important conditions are then subtracted as void spaces. Firstly, the main streets and squares that define the building clusters and then secondary paths and yards for pedestrians that cross inside the clusters. **1.25** New ground conditions in the residential tower blocks. **1.26** Void studies. **1.27** Sectional perspective. **1.28** Axonometric view of cluster. Each cluster has an external and internal condition. The external condition refers to the greater Algiers and the internal condition to the local economy and production. While the two systems are distinct, they interact on multiple levels so that small workshops have the opportunity to grow from the interior to the exterior, and bigger companies have the chance to get involved with local activities.

1.28

Athens

2

Athens Beyond Urbanisation

Yannis Aesopos, Ross Exo Adams

To approach any city within the Mediterranean today requires a precise, critical and constrained position, critical both with respect to the material we research, but also to our own methods as urbanists. For us, it is important to reject the journalistic impulse to capture a certain 'dynamic present' characterised by the spectacle of crisis we constantly see in the images reproduced in newspapers on a daily basis. In that same way, we also reject the flattening of the complexities and politics of Athens into an endless parade of mappings, data and information-for-information's-sake, which has become the architectural status quo of urban research today. In rejecting these approaches, we choose to understand Athens strictly through a rigorous archaeology of its material formation, that is to say, through an archaeology of its urbanisation.

By 'urbanisation', we do not mean simply the production of the built environment or the growth of the city over time and space. Rather, we mean to identify both a process and a logic in which the concrete order of space and form is itself the basis from which political, economic, social and material conditions are created and mediated – the very same conditions whose effects are captured in the images of mass media or mapped in the drawings of architects and urbanists. Urbanisation is itself the medium which both results from and causes crisis; it is the process which perverts the notions of public and private alike; it is the activity which itself brings the theatre of war into permanent contact with society; it is the process which uses historical artefacts in order to flatten history into a consumable image; it is a spatial logic which attempts to reduce life itself into an economic calculation of private property and circulation, consumption and production, dwellings and infrastructure.

We claim that only by developing an archaeology of urbanisation – through a deep understanding of the concrete morphology of the city as well as the legal, political and economic mechanisms of its particular mode of reproduction – we are able to construct a different history of Athens, one which immediately goes beyond the spectacle of crisis as well as the pomp of data. This approach for us is already a project in itself.

Athens exists today as both a symptom of a generalised condition and a unique paradigm: it is the site of a form of urbanisation that took place in the postwar period that was both generic and specific. It was based on the infinite repetition, in numerous variations, of the multi-programmatic building type of the polykatoikia (apartment building), the city's 'urban unit'. The polykatoikia stands as the material outcome of unique economic and legal mechanisms, still in place today. Its realisation was made possible through the system of 'antiparochi', the exchange of land for a number of future apartments, within a standard building type whose form is controlled by the General Building Regulation. Contrary to what took place in other western European countries, the Greek state chose not to be involved in the production of housing, handling the entire field over to the small-to-medium sized private contractors, the builders of the polykatoikias. The continuous layer of polykatoikias covered the pre-existing natural environment and realised a 'private urbanisation' that paid little attention to public space, which remained a residue of the private.

This form of urbanisation, devoid of theory or planning schemes, continued uninterrupted through all the post-war years until the construction works for the Athens 2004 Olympic Games began in the late 1990s. The Olympic projects, along with several other major infrastructure projects that were built during the same period, co-funded by the European Union, can all be seen as a very ambitious modernisation 'package'. In effect, what they did was to lay the ground for the superimposition, a second urbanisation layer of a more generic or global type, one not based on domesticity, but rather on large-scale infrastructures of circulation: airport, highways, Metro, light-rail and tram networks. The new mobility provided by circulation networks and easy credit offered by the increasingly globalised banking system within the booming, however uncontrolled, Eurozone economy, quickly led to the development of an intense consumerist culture throughout the Attica region and the abandonment of city-centre public spaces – spaces that gradually became occupied by the thousands of precarious migrants whose exceptional legal status forced them to call Athens their home. The city's diffusion along the new networks into the surrounding Attica region was marked by new, ever-larger shopping centres. Social and economic crisis did not take long to emerge. In such a context, traditional practices of urban design are put into question. As designers, we seek to open up new, radical and politicised modes of intervention; we locate our work as openings within the urban condition, spaces which open out to a world beyond the political and spatial inevitability of the urban.

We would like to extend our thanks for the invaluable input from: Andreas Angelidakis, Aristide Antonas, Petros Babasikas, Harris Biskos, Dimitris Christopoulos, Panos Dragonas, Orsalia Dimitrou, Jonathan Hill, Platon Issaias, Sam Jacoby, Dimitra Katsota, Andreas Kourkoulas, Marina Lathouri, Kieran Long, John Palmesino, Daniel Fernandez Pascual, Godofredo Pereira, Angelo Plessas, Charles Rice, Douglas Spencer, Nikos Xydakis, Yiorgis Yerolymbos, Thanos Zartaloudis and Elia Zenghelis.

We would also like to thank the Benaki Museum, Athens and its Director, Professor Angelos Delivorias, for their hospitality in providing workshop space within the Museum during our field trip to Athens.

Students
Chrysanthe Constantinou, Ting Ding, Yunzhu Guo, Yishan Li, Jing Lin, Bin Liu, Ye Qingmin, Lavanya Venugopal, Lirong Wang, Ya Wang, Zilong Yang, Xi Zhang

N

0   2.5   5   10km

2.1

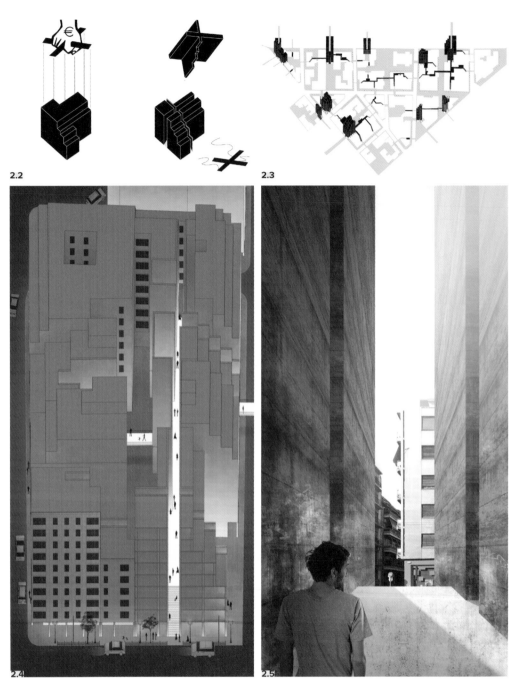

2.2

2.3

2.4

2.5

2.1 Athens Attica map, group work **2.2 – 2.7 Bin Liu**
Uselessness of Private Property. Urbanisation from the 1990s
onwards was always accompanied by deterritorialisation of
debt. Due to the recent economic crisis which started in
2008, the amount of Greece's governmental debt increased
dramatically; the country became the biggest debtor in the
Mediterranean basin. As a result of the gloomy economy and
the unpayable debt, an increasing number of polykatoikias in
the centre of Athens were abandoned. What if those private
properties are somehow disabled, taken out of the economic
circle? To stimulate further thinking about private property and
debt, the project proposes to get rid of the profitable part of
these abandoned real estate properties by crudely performing
physical 'cuts' on nine selected abandoned polykatoikias in the

city centre. The resulting improperly-sized buildings create a
suspended, 'blurry' status of private property while breaking
the boundaries between public and private space, usefulness
and uselessness. **2.2** Diagram of intervention. Since the
interior size of the abandoned buildings which have been
crudely cut cannot meet the minimal requirement necessary
for property transaction, these properties are no longer
involved in the economic circle of private property. **2.3**
Conceptual drawing. It not only represents the relationship
between each single abandoned building and the block it's
allocated, but also shows a new network across blocks by
cutting those abandoned buildings and releasing vacant
spaces. **2.4** Axonometric rendering (detail). The axonometric
rendering from a particular angle clearly shows the way the

2.6

2.7

abandoned building is cut and how the cuts extend in the entire block and even across blocks. **2.5** The corridor space between two solid walls not only divides the abandoned building into parts but also blurs the boundary between private and public, usefulness and uselessness. **2.6** Detail of cutting. The nine axonometric renderings above show how the abandoned buildings are cut by concrete walls and how people access these buildings (through stairs and corridors). The combined section drawing below represents public spaces existing within masses of private property. **2.7** Axonometric rendering (overall). Light and shadow in this night rendering could help to clarify the new spaces created by cutting abandoned real estate properties from 'solid' private spaces. The path of light represents the extension of these public spaces. The distribution of people in the rendering shows the adjusted boundary between public and private.

2.8

2.9

2.10

2.8 – 2.13 Jing Lin Beyond the Stage. This project examines public spaces in Athens as institutions. In recent years public spaces have supported capitalist interests and have been turned into symbolic stages of violent acts during the crisis. The project intends to explore the possibility of public space going beyond the stage and acting as a representation of new political form and the concrete spaces in which new assemblies can manifest. The main design strategy is to use walls to withdraw these spaces from their conventional way of operating within the city and to create new spaces of multiple scales for multiple interactions. The walls are not only tools of deconstruction but also function as boundaries, spaces and frames. Three squares were chosen as case studies. **2.8** Site map. The public today is not fixed but flexible and mobile,

bound to public action. This project investigates the possibility of a public diffused within the whole of urban space, indifferent to the division between interior and exterior. In this sense, the urban no longer consists of solid architectures and circulation systems, but instead of a flat surface divided by walls. The previously planned public spaces, as a provocation of institution of representation, could become the dramatic representation of the new political form but which is a complex of living theatres with the coexistence of different wills. **2.9** Axonometric drawing of Syntagma Square. The shifting of axis from the direction of the House of Parliament to the direction of pedestrian entrances emphasises the concentration of different scales of interaction from big assemblies to small group meetings. **2.10** Living theatre in Syntagma Square. The

interruption of the view to the House of Parliament turns the characters of performers and audience around and stimulated the awareness of the passers-by as an audience. **2.11** Space in the wall, Syntagma Square. The space in the wall is a transition between two kinds of spaces and a void within the city. **2.12** Axonometric drawing of Klafthmonos Square. The walls act as spaces for both circulation and stasis. **2.13** Outdoor cinema, Klafthmonos Square. The most theatrical space on this site, large stairs connect the cafe above and the lower lawn with the blank wall as background. There is platform on the top of the wall communicating with the cafe at the same level.

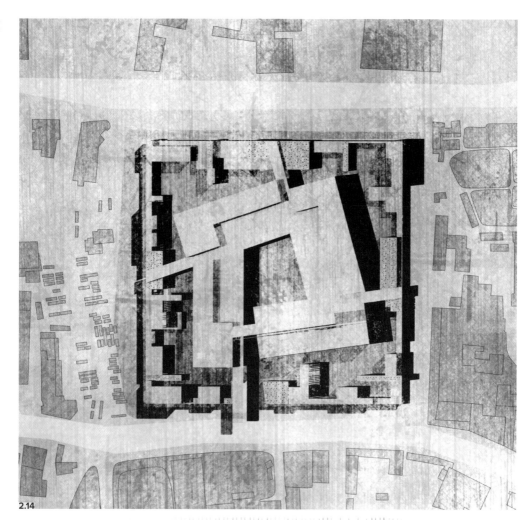

2.14

2.15

2.14 – 2.17 Chrysanthe Constantinou Beyond Waste: Excess as a Political Platform. The project concentrates on a specific subjectivity created by our modern heritage: illegal recyclers and scavengers, the marginal figures of waste – people who are excluded from the mainstream economic system and the state's regulations, while they are still employed within the capitalist mode of value production. The city of Athens is the platform for this exploration, uncovering a city's waste which is recycled by thousands of people that live in the margins of law; a recycling process which serves a huge industrial production and which further brokers the proliferation of capital; a recycling which, at the same time, reproduces the same 'exceptional' conditions. By creating an autonomous platform of operation which expresses and articulates this exceptional

state of being, the project seeks to embrace the political significance of these subjectivities whose 'life is released from the law, but, despite the civil death this implies, they are also, potentially, and, in an extreme manner, the potential ground of a new law, or, more provocatively, the potential to be a law unto oneself'.

2.16

2.17

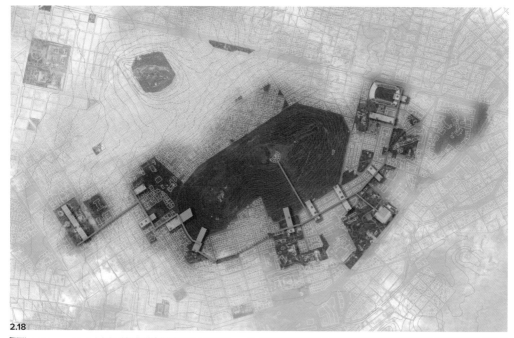

2.18

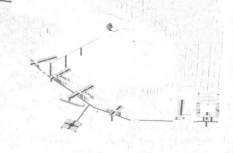

2.20

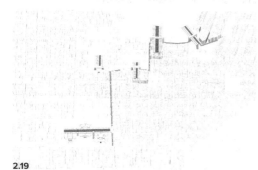

2.19

2.21

2.18 – 2.21 Xi Zhang Reconstructed Nature. Athens' urban landscape is a carpet of polykatoikias with scattered natural looking 'voids' of hills. These voids were formed in the process of Athens' urbanisation and are defined as 'constructed nature' in this study. The project developed around one of the 'constructed nature' sites, the hill of Lycabettus. It is made of two parts: a network of passageways and a series of roof gardens. The network combines the green open spaces around the hill and the hill itself. On top of this network are the roof gardens which flow into the city and can be seen as a 'new ground' of the city. The aim of the project is to rebuild the relationship between nature and the urban. **2.18** Masterplan. The project connects the green space around Lycabettus hill to the hill itself. At the same time, the roof

gardens become a new 'natural ground' in the urban. **2.19** Roof gardens. Under each of the roof gardens there are some buildings, most of which are important public buildings of the specific area. **2.20** The roof garden on the axis line of the Acropolis and Lycabettus hills. **2.21** The roof garden above the Panathinaikos Stadium.

2.22

2.23

2.24

2.22 – 2.24 Lirong Wang After Public Space Framework for a Potential Common. The prevailing privatisations – spatial domination, policing, and surveillance – of the civic life of Athens has led to the decline of its public space. Public spaces have become an arena for an increasing number of protests and demonstrations that often take a violent and destructive form. At the same time, the mushrooming of social urban movements trigger the potential to construct and inhabit new forms of social relations – embracing the common as a means to negotiate the conflict between the governing and the governed, instead of a simple rejection or confrontation. This project attempts to explore the possibility of common space – a space beyond the binary opposition of public and private, using the façade as a principle tool to transform and unify the existing urban fabric: street and square. A resulting continuous series of loggias and chambers will unfold in the whole city to achieve the sense of commonality. **2.22** Overall axonometric. Located in a highly mixed-use district, the new framework pierces through the street and squares in between, forging common experiences in different scales. **2.23** Detail axonometric. The loggia is divided into different partitions not for circulation, but for the common experience for different groups. It contributes to form not only the physical common, which takes the form of the homogenous façade, but also a social common place for the inhabitants and workers of the blocks. **2.24** Chamber in Karaiskaki Square. Although born in ancient public squares, the chambers possess another meaning to the city and its civic life today.

2.25

2.26

2.25 – 2.29 Lavanya Venugopal Traces of Movement: The Spatial Abstraction of Political Treaties in Europe. The project problematises Athens as a region of transit in the geopolitical scale of Mediterranean migration and seeks to make explicit this highly politicised issue. By trying to make permanent something which is by essence ephemeral, the project aims to reveal a certain paradox at the heart of the contemporary treatment of migration in Europe. It delves into the process of migration through the rigour of archiving a subjectivity and creating a platform to lend scale and meaning to the phases of the many journeys that have led people around the world to wind up in Athens. The ground plays a powerful symbolic as well as material role in the project. It represents a dimension of Athens, rich in archaeological significance, and conveys a great

deal about populations and civilisations it encapsulates. It also represents the hidden, the past, and the repressed.
2.25 Archive entrance. **2.26** Archive interior. **2.27** Archive Interior **2.28 – 2.29** Settlement. The settlement constitutes the living archive of a community and an urban register of people capable of developing over a period of time. Through an introverted design layout of housing, community gathering spaces are created in the civic realm, offering long-term quality spaces for resettlement as an alternative to the detention of so called hospitality centres.

2.27

2.28

2.29

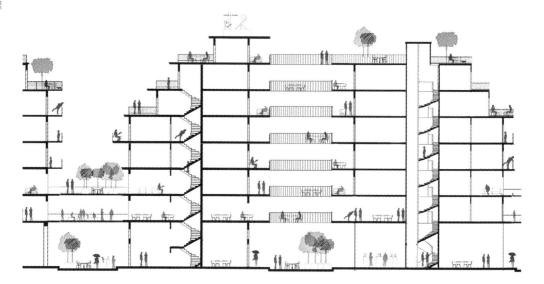

2.33

2.34

2.35

2.33 – 2.35 Ting Ding The New Form of Collectivity. The project starts with the controversial debate on the appropriate reaction to the contemporary urban issue of 'identity crisis': in what way should we comprehend the notion of collectivity and collective identity and how should urban space respond to this crucial issue? Taking Athens as a paradigm, this project intends to challenge the present network of social space in contemporary urban areas in general. Regarding the 'sea' of high-density polykatoikia as a latent project for free and diverse human interactions to take place, the strategy of this project is to introduce possible new social formations by intervening in the spatial relation between indoor intimate space and outdoor common space. **2.33** Concept section. The original interior intimate spaces of the private dwelling will be reorganised by

the introduction of a new network of common spaces set out according to various densities of human interactions. **2.34** First floor plan. The new first floor plan shows the close relationship between indoor intimate space and outdoor common space, cultivating the emergence of new forms of social relations. **2.35** Model photo showing the system of original polykatoikia (MDF board) together with the newly built platform and corridor (transparent Perspex) and the recuperated common 'rooms' (white Perspex).

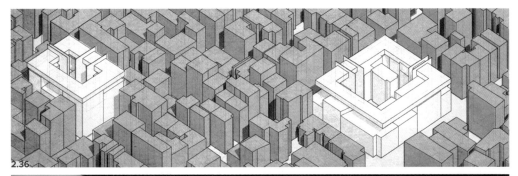

2.36

2.37

2.38

2.36 – 2.38 Yunzhu Guo Against Domestic City. The polykatoikia can be read as both the cause and the effect in the urbanisation of modern Athens. Urbanisation was realised through the system of 'antiparochi' – the exchange between land properties and built dwellings – without money involved. This process met the massive demand for living space and stimulated further infinite domestic expansion resulting in a lack of public space. Athens can be regarded as an absolute domestic city. The project proposes an intervention in the polykatoikia in order to suggest the possibility for a new public within the domestic realm. The project aims to break through the currently closed-off urban block, connecting its interior to the surrounding streets and injecting public programmes throughout. By the insertion of new dwellings on top of the existing buildings, the rooftop space becomes a potential for commonality as the possible interaction between old and new. **2.36** Concept. **2.37** Strategy. **2.38** The gesture of the wall cutting through the block indicates the public has been permitted into what was formerly the domestic realm, which opens up a new procedure against domestic city.

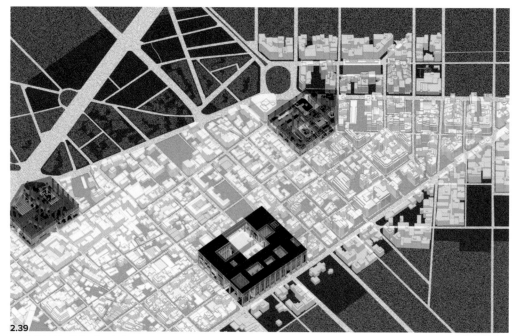

2.39

2.40

2.41

2.39 – 2.44 Ya Wang The Battery: A Production Centre in Athens. The Battery is about intensification. It seeks to condense all aspects of urban life into a unified environment: working, living, education, sports, multicultural activities, shopping, hotel and religious space. From an architectural point of view, it also aims to integrate several blocks of fragmented buildings into a whole, dramatising the confrontation between the new mega-block and the context of individual polykatoikias. The Battery is also about production. Situated in a traditional productive area in central Athens, it intends to retrieve the urban character of a production centre by identifying a working community. During a time when 'crisis' has become the inevitable cliché for Greece and even the entire Mediterranean, the Battery

aims to actualise the potential for the renewal of the city centre and to provide a new spatial concept for the urban. **2.39** Concept drawing. Situated in the concrete forest of small-scale polykatoikias in the historical centre, the self-sufficient island is in pronounced contrast to its surroundings. **2.40 – 2.41** Model showing existing buildings and additions. **2.42** Section 1. Introduction of collective housing as a new layer above the existing buildings creates spatial richness between the two, transforming the abandoned roof-tops into spaces for public cultural activities. **2.43** Section 2. **2.44** West elevation.

2.42

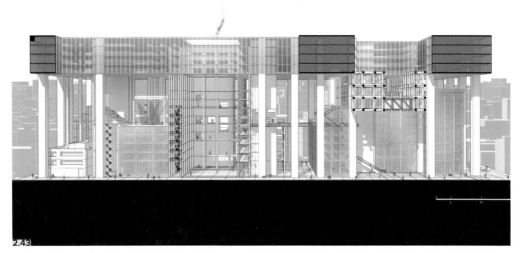

2.43

2.44

2.45

2.46

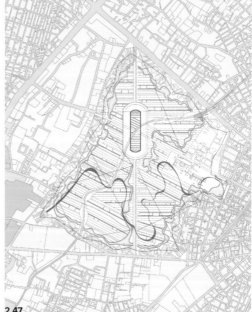

2.47

2.45 Ye Qingmin Grids as Residue. The grids have long been an apparatus of urbanisation. They are not only a form for the city to reproduce itself, but also to inform a specific way of life for people. This apparatus has been deeply influenced by the economic and political factors often hidden from view. This project proposes a strategy to reconceptualise the grid as an adhesive against the dispersive forces of urbanisation. It aims to use the grid as a counter apparatus to the existing gridded space of Athens, redefining the private and public, inside and outside, and giving a new relationship between the infrastructure and communities it surrounds. Axonometric of the bay site where the grid becomes more solid, containing housing and office programmes. **2.46 – 2.47 Yishan Li** This project aims to infiltrate agricultural activities into Athens' city planning, seeing it as a beneficial factor of city function and introducing agriculture to the public policy of urban space in order to research the relationship between agriculture and the city. It points out that the combination of agriculture and cities can form a new closed self-circulation urban development pattern. If agriculture is to return to the city, it first should be committed to utilising all kinds of negative space in the urban fabric. **2.46** Concept drawing. **2.47** Masterplan. The structure of the whole park is composed of four parts, the green plant network (farmland, woodland, grassland), the blue stream network (river, wetland, fish pond), the transportation network (landscape axis avenue, skywalk, fast road, art gallery) and the research and production centre.

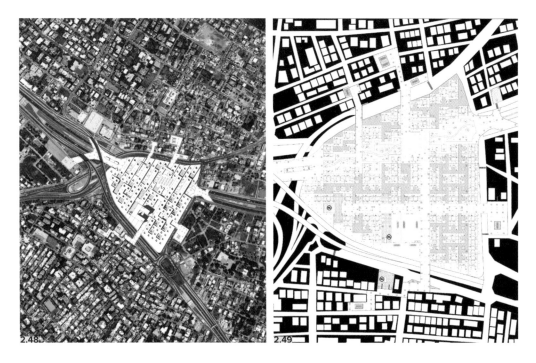

2.48

2.49

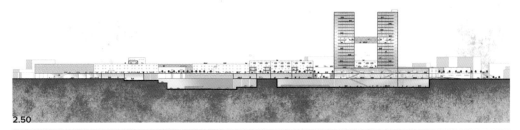

2.50

2.51

2.48 – 2.51 Zilong Yang Node City. The network has become a common logic of urbanisation used in the current urban planning. Generic spaces are dominated by the movements of capital, channeled along corridors and into the nodes of the network, and thus are often lifeless, and transient. This project takes the opportunity to redesign the space of a node in Athens' periphery. The project explores the possibility of reinterpreting this space, consisting of a transit hub, shopping mall, social housing and a public park, designed as a mega-structure. **2.48** Site Plan. The node is made up of small-scale units which are of a similar scale to the polykatoikia nearby. It has an island character to make explicit its function as a node, but does not remain closed. Public life happens on the extension of the node as well as in its interior. **2.49** First floor plan. Housing is the main element on the first floor. The space above the previous metro station is shaped as a core transit centre of the project. And the Attiki Odos highway is covered and transformed into a highway park serving the surrounding communities. **2.50** Concept Section. The section shows the multiple layers of the project. The mat housing forms, together with the highway park, respond to urban, contextual and spatial conditions in Athens, while the twin towers are visible from the city centre, giving a sense of scale and place to what is otherwise abstract and dimensionless. **2.51** Highway Park. The park is located on top of the Attiki Odos highway. It serves not only the people inside the node but also those from outside. A new public space is created.

Beirut

3

The Privatisation of the Public: The Architecture of Education

Aristide Antonas, Sam Jacoby

The Beirut studio started with this crucial observation: one of the most challenging aspects of the city is its idiosyncratic fragmentation. In response, students defined delicate possibilities of unifying different areas in the city that could operate without disturbing their existing limits. We insisted on two major factors that could affect this: public transport and education. Consequently, we proposed a new tramway system and worked on an educational spine (including university facilities, museums and exhibition halls) that would follow the Green Line from the sea to the south of the city, creating a hospitable common ground for all different communities of the city.

Despite a recent history of factionalism, Beirut's 5,000 years of continuous inhabitation and urbanisation arguably bear witness to an even longer history of complex coexistence. Strategically located on the Mediterranean coast at the connecting point of the European, Asian, and African continents, it was shaped by successive and concurrent Phoenician, Hellenistic, Roman, Byzantine, Crusader, Arab, and Ottoman influences.

Yet Beirut's urban and cultural importance at different times and for different political and economic reasons is not fully understood without considering the formative role that education and knowledge has played in establishing it as an important intellectual, liberal, and cosmopolitan centre. The Law School of Berytus, allegedly the most important in the Roman Empire until the city's destruction by an earthquake in 551, is an early case in point. A later urban renaissance that established Beirut as a primary centre in the Levant was impossible without the influence by foreign missionaries but only came to full fruition in the second half of the nineteenth century with complementary Ottoman reforms and new Arabic educational institutions, which together resulted in a defining modernisation of society. This created one of the densest educational networks in the region and, although a source of protonationalism, equally fostered pluralism and international relations. Today, as advisor to the Ministry of Education Maha Shuayb argues, education remains essential in Lebanon: firstly to create social cohesion, relational justice, and equality of access, and then to bring about critical citizenship – important steps to overcoming crippling confessionalism. Thus, we can posit that the sociopolitical dimensions of education and knowledge are essential in constructing futures for Beirut and challenging historical and sectarian divisions that are embedded in the comprehension of the city.

This raises the question of how to spatialise education and consider the interrelated scales that define Beirut in terms relevant to urban design: the scale of architecture, its specificity and typological analysis; the urban scale, its configuration, limits and centralities but also the political and socio-economic realities that organise it; the national scale, Beirut's role in the building of a nation state or as a capital city; the regional scale, its economic and geopolitical meanings to the Arab World and the Mediterranean and European Union.

The enquiries emerging from these different scales were the starting point to reconsider the dichotomy of public and private that underlies the discipline of urban design, and led to an examination of how different stakeholders and constituencies affect the formation of an urban plan. This influence is evident in the impact that two main private institutions of higher learning had on Beirut's urban form. The Syrian Protestant College, today known as the American University of Beirut and founded by American missionaries in 1866, shaped the western growth of the city towards Hamra. While its interiorised and highly secured campus physically dominates and defines a district, it also has been formative to the sociocultural richness of the surrounding area and increased public and economic activity. The Collège of the Jesuits, founded in 1875 and today's Université Saint-Joseph, had a comparable, albeit less obvious, effect on the eastern area of Achrafieh. Both universities are closely related to two important lines of urban growth, the coastal Corniche and Damascus Road, which links the former Syrian port of Beirut with Damascus.

The difficulty in conceptualising the public and provide public spaces and infrastructures is especially apparent in Beirut, with its long tradition of relying on private initiatives and investment for their provision. Unsurprisingly, the postwar reconstruction of the city centre is carried out by a private real estate management company, Solidere, with special powers of eminent domain and regulatory authority – controls usually held by the state. Nevertheless, this does not make Beirut an exception but an example of an increasingly common global form of urban development, in which public projects are privatised and large-scale private projects replace the role of governmental masterplans.

We thank all our jurors. Special thanks to Yasmina El Chami, Sakiko Goto, Fadi Mansour and Yuwei Wang, for their valuable insights and dedicated workshops. We are grateful to Maha Shuayb from the Centre for Lebanese Studies for her lecture and Robert Saliba at the American University of Beirut for his assistance.

Students
Eleftheria Androulakaki, Xinlei Gong, Dongbo Han, Xiaoying (Sean) Wan, Meng Xu, Yilei Xu, Miao Yu, Jingyang Zhai, Jie Zhu

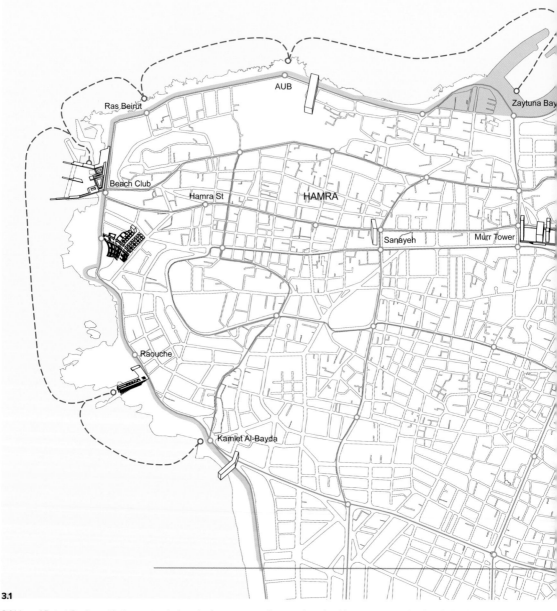

3.1

3.1 Map of Beirut. Dealing with the previously described realities and challenges, the students studied three urban lines. First, the coast and the Corniche as a driver of urban development, which also provide a public refuge that is seen as a space of neutrality and coexistence by Beirutis. Protected by legislation for the common good and from private development since 1896, the coastal line is continuously 'violated' by privatisation. Second, the Green Line, formed during the civil war from 1975 to 1990 along Damascus Road, an urban manifestation of conflict but also an important north-south growth axis of the city that goes back to ancient times. The former Green Line links the city centre and two of the historically most important civic spaces, Martyrs' Square and the park Horsh Al-Sanawbar. Its redevelopment is predominantly realised by private capital and includes the city centre managed by Solidere. And third, the tramway lines, first opened in 1909 but dysfunctional since the civil war, which, although built by a private company, provided a large-scale public transport infrastructure and was part of the urban regularisation of Beirut. Based on these studies, an interrelated urban strategy was devised that proposed a metropolitan infrastructure consisting of a combined network of public transportation and educational-cultural institutions as providers of new public facilities and spaces that serve the larger city and local residents. Some of these nodes were subsequently developed individually as examples of how urban design and architectural ambitions can become an integral part of a larger urban vision.

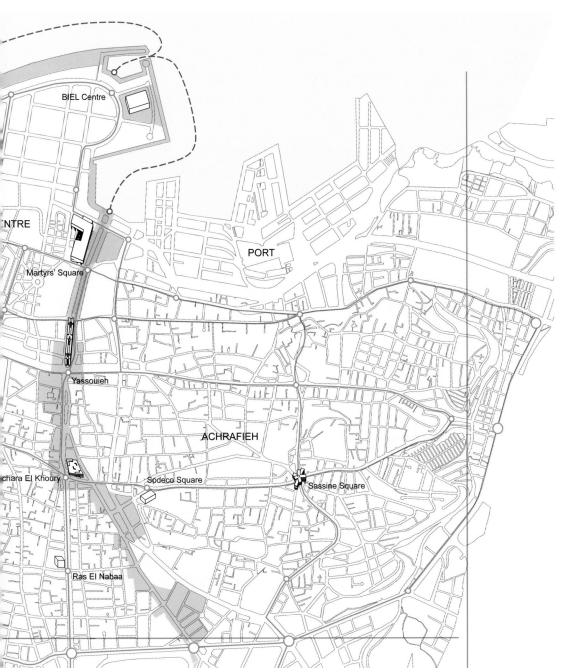

BIEL Centre

NTRE

Martyrs' Square

PORT

Yassouieh

ACHRAFIEH

chara El Khoury

Sodeco Square

Sassine Square

Ras El Nabaa

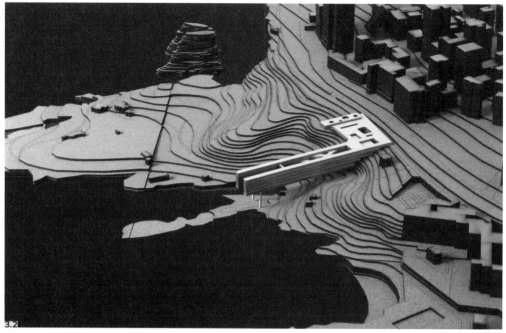

3.2

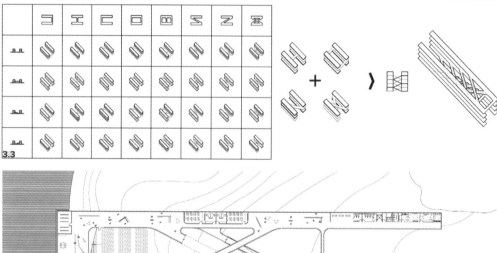

3.3

3.4

3.2 – 3.7 Xiaoying (Sean) Wan The Corniche as Urban Extension. A perpendicular extension to Beirut's Corniche creates a new public realm for the Beirutis that is part of an urban and public infrastructure, connected by tramway and water bus. Inserted into the slope of the steep coast, it spatially extends to and visually frames the sea, while programmatically becoming more than just a seaside promenade by providing diverse public functions (artist studios, art gallery, and an art school). These enhance growing local art-based activities and support a wide range of existing informal, public activities in Raouche and the landmark views of the Pigeons' Rock. It is a new refuge that opportunistically reinterprets and extends the neutrality associated with the Corniche. **3.2** Model view of proposal in Raouche. **3.3** Transformation of linearly arranged

corridor types in section (common in gallery and school types). **3.4** Typical building plan of 'three-dimensional Corniche' showing the art gallery and artist studios. **3.5** Site and landscape plan. **3.6** Cross-section. **3.7** Axonometric view of proposal.

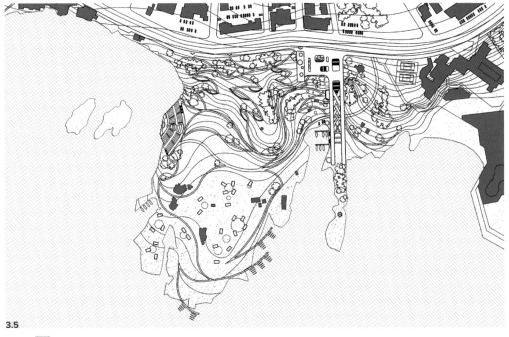

3.5

3.6

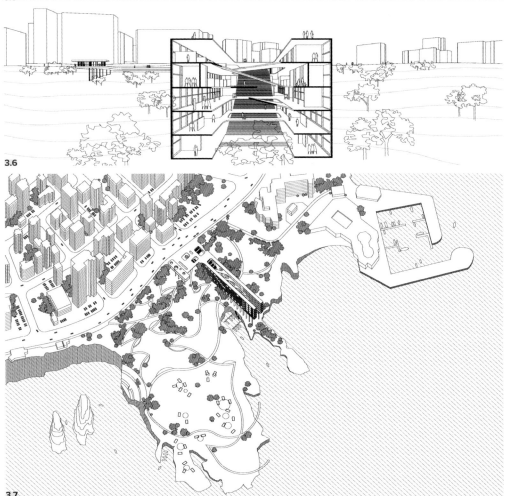

3.7

3.8

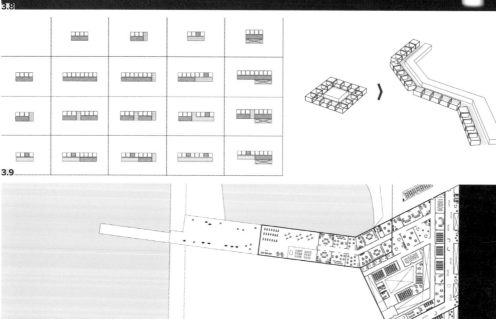

3.9

3.10

3.8 – 3.13 Meng Xu Public Beach Club. The Corniche in Beirut is the possibility to rethink the access to and protection of the common, with the Corniche also referring to a common Mediterranean project and desires. Located at the main entrance point from the city to the sea, the site of the proposal can be regarded as an important centre at the edge of Beirut. To replace the existing 'wall' around the site, which blocks views and access to the common sea, the proposed public beach club creates a new infrastructure along the Corniche. This addresses the lacking public beach facilities in the city and makes the beach accessible to different users and their requirements: swimming centre, spa, beach resort, leisure pools, and a sports secondary school. The new beach club is articulated as a series of linear buildings that define the separation and connection between private and public areas – maintaining the privacy of the army beach to the north and the courtyards of the new secondary schools, while creating porous transitions between the varous public beach facilities within the club. **3.8** Model view of the public beach club. **3 9** Transformation of couryard to linear wall type. **3.10** Typical plan showing transition from linear (beach club) to courtyard arrangement (secondary school). **3.11** Site and landscape plan. **3.12** Cross-section and elevation. **3.13** Axonometric view of proposal.

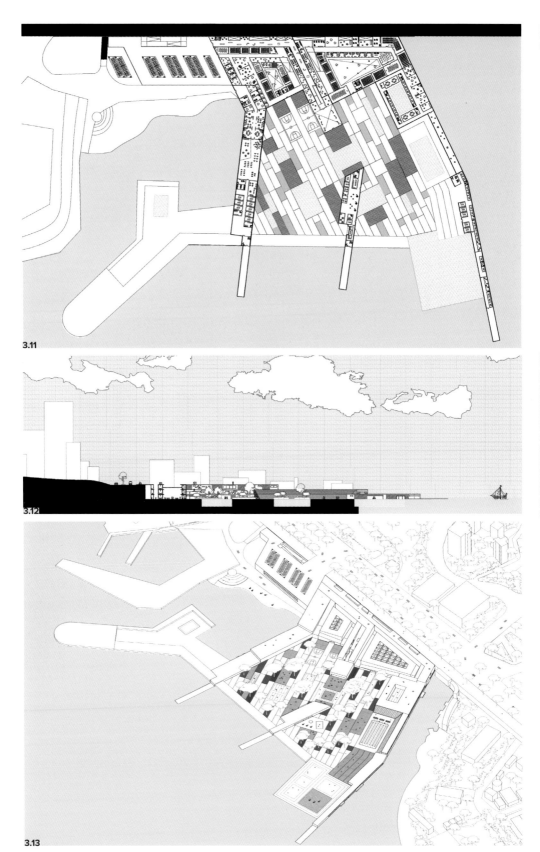

3.11

3.12

3.13

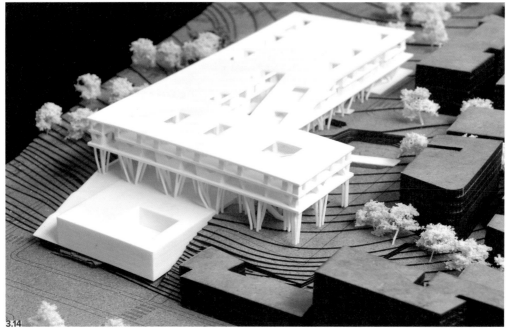

3.14

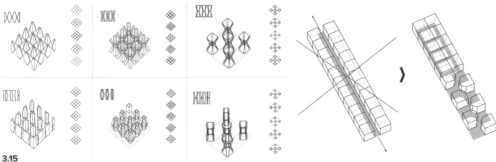

3.15

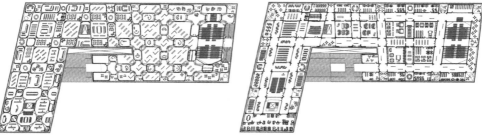

3.16

3.14 – 3.19 Miao Yu National Archaeological Research Centre. This project is proposed as a hybrid infrastructure functioning as a cultural and educational focal point in the city centre of Beirut. Located above one of the most ancient and important archaeological sites in Beirut – the end of the former 'Green Line' and next to Martyrs' Square – the archaeological research centre is conceived as a new public space with the aim to reconfigure and integrate diverse activities by different social groups through culture and knowledge. At the same time, the proposal memorialises a multi-layered visible and invisible national history. Based on the corridor type found in the educational buildings, the conventional room-to-corridor / private-to-public relationship is transformed into an 'enfilade type' by merging and off-setting cellular units. 'Rooms' are

redefined that programmatically create a hybridity of diverse activities and offer possibilities for unexpected experience and social encounters. **3.14** Model view of the archaeological research centre. **3.15** Transformation of corridor to enfilade type. **3.16** First and second floor plan showing the sectional transition of structure and room / cell types. **3.17** Site and archaeological plan. **3.18** Longitudinal section. **3.19** Axonometric view of proposal.

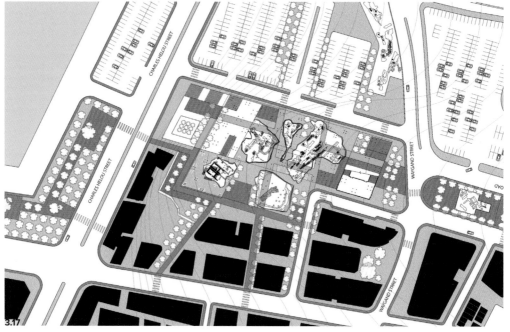

3.17

3.18

3.19

3.20

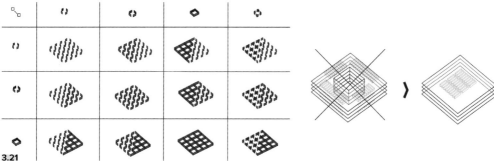

3.21

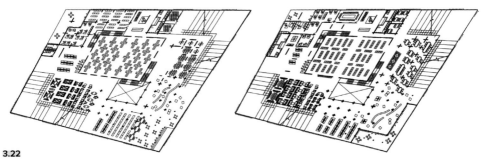

3.22

3.20 – 3.25 Xinlei Gong National Library. Within the proposed cultural belt of the former Green Line, the new National Library of Lebanon emphasises public activities and leisure beyond the traditional library function: gardens, kindergarten, markets, and meeting and play areas. The library is seen as a place of social encounter, providing besides conventional study and research areas additional spaces for public debates and entertainment. Consequently, the typical plan of a library as an enclosed space with bookshelves arranged around a central void is inverted, with the library functions now taking place in a 'private' centre surrounded by light and open spaces for public activities. The cellular arrangement of the public library into private and public areas is transformed into a gradient of publicness. **3.20** Model view of the National Library.

3.21 Transformation of interiorised to exteriorised library plan formed by porous sectional modules. **3.22** First and second floor plan showing the sectional transition and articulation of the public realm around the library core. **3.23** Site and landscape plan. **3.24** Cross-section. **3.25** Axonometric view of proposal.

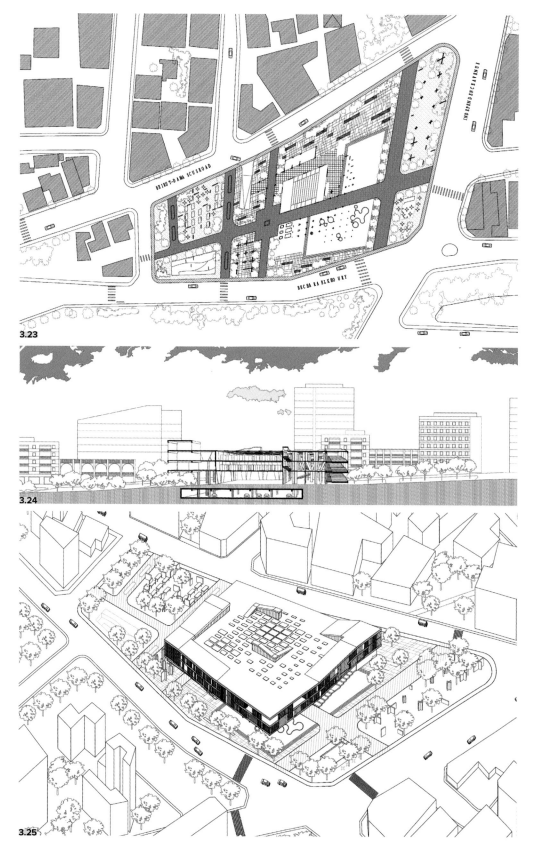

3.23

3.24

3.25

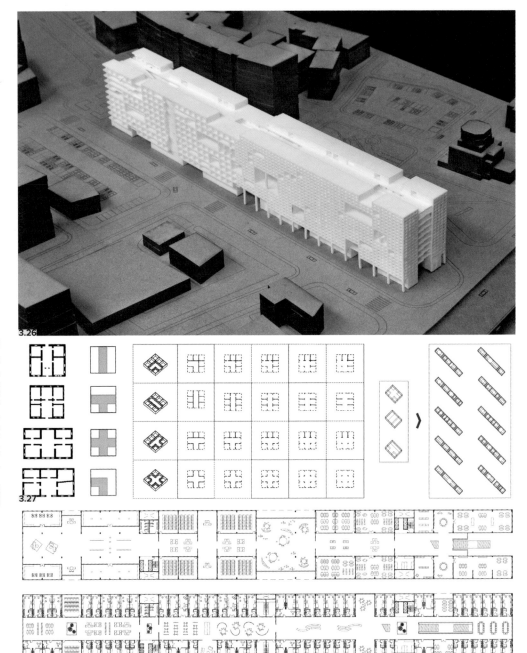

3.26

3.27

3.28

3.26 – 3.31 Jie Zhu Student Housing. This project proposes student housing for the Lebanese University and Université Saint-Joseph within the centre that is otherwise reserved for high-end housing. The site is located south of Martyr's Square and north of the ringroad around the city centre. Based on the typical Lebanese housing type – the central hall type – the project reinterprets the central hall as common and shared spaces that function at the urban and building scale. As part of the cultural belt, it provides a public ground and three-dimensional public hall that cuts through all levels of the building and leads to the public roof. At the building scale, all facilities and learning and study areas shared by students are also placed within smaller and more intimate central halls, offering a variety of activities and spaces on each floor level.

The central hall thus becomes a differentiated space for common and social activities, a space of encounter. **3.26** Model view of the student housing. **3.27** Transformation of the vernacular central hall type into a slab block with central halls forming public and shared (common) space at different building and urban scales. **3.28** First and second floor plan showing the varying size of central hall arrangments. **3.29** Site plan. **3.30** Longitudinal section. **3.31** Axonometric view.

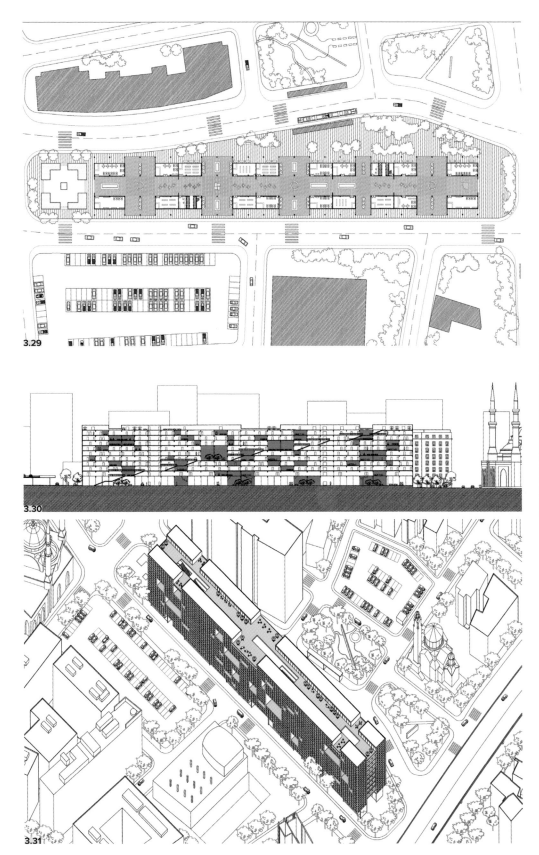

3.29

3.30

3.31

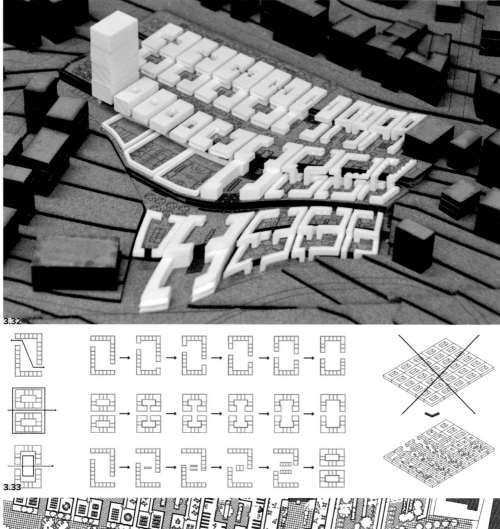

3.32

3.33

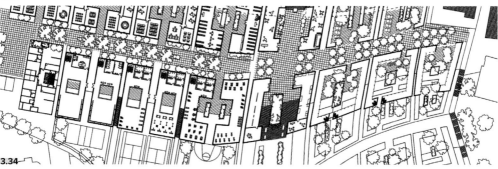

3.34

3.32 – 3.37 Yilei Xu Sports Academy (Lebanese University). Part of the proposed dispersed urban campus of the Lebanese University linked by a new tramway network, the project is for a sports academy in Ras Beirut. The site is a popular local route leading to the Cornice and coast. To accommodate the sports academy and provide amenities for the local residents, a series of overlapping and linked courtyards are created that form a network of public and private gardens. The private gardens are enclosed by the academy buildings and contain the sports fields, whereas the public gardens are framed by colonnades and lead down to the coast and the tramway station. Following the model of a private-public partnership, parts of the site are reserved for high-rise and high-end housing, to accommodate already

existing development plans and make the private sector a stakeholder in the governmental and institutional development. **3.32** Model view of the sports academy. **3.33** Transformation of typical educational courtyard types into a differentiated grid and mat of connected courtyards. **3.34** Typical strip showing the transition from enclosed and programmed to open and landscaped courtyards. **3.35** Site and landscape plan. **3.36** Cross-section. **3.37** Axonometric view.

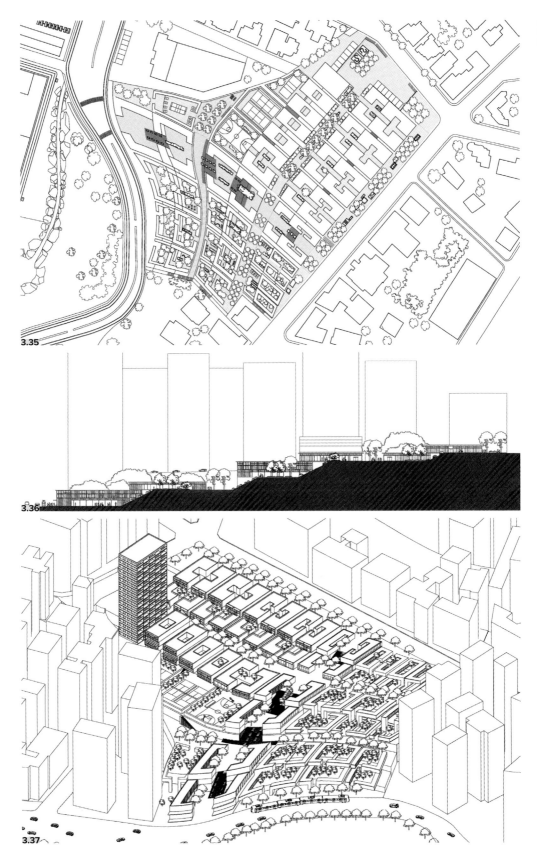

3.35

3.36

3.37

3.38

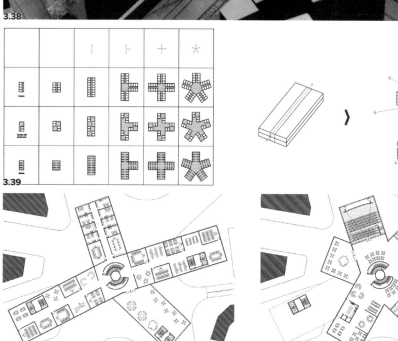

3.39

3.40

3.38 – 3.43 Dongbo Han Business School (Lebanese University). Also part of the proposed tramway network and Lebanese University campus, this is a design for a business school in Achrafiyeh. Situated above one of the main traffic nodes at Sassine Square, the proposal consists of the school at its lower levels, a public section with a cinema and circulation level in the middle, which is linked to the two tramway stations below, and private housing above. The integration of housing by a private developer is part of the funding strategy and allows a mix of stakeholders while delivering a project for the general public, the academic user, and the private resident. **3.38** Model view of the business school above the traffic island. **3.39** Transformation of the linear corridor and enfilade types into a radial organisation.

3.40 Second (business school) and fourth (cinema) floor plan. **3.41** Typical plan (housing, sixth floor) **3.42** Cross-section. **3.43** Axonometric view.

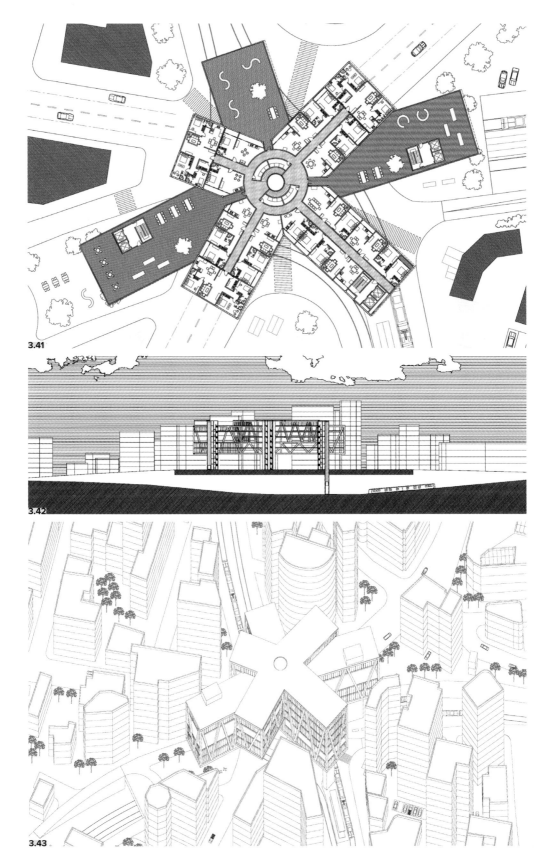

3.41

3.42

3.43

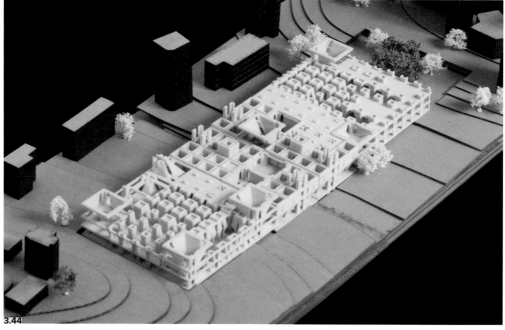

3.44

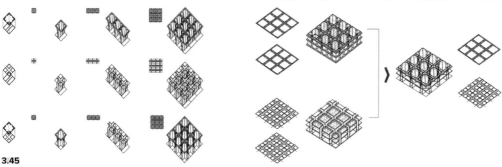

3.45

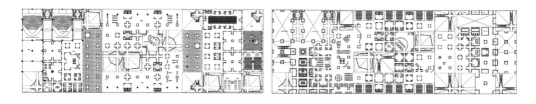

3.46

3.44 – 3.49 Jingyang Zhai Faculty of Middle Eastern Studies (Lebanese University) Based on the proposal for an urban campus, the design project is for the faculty of Middle Eastern studies of the Lebanese University. Besides the main programme, other facilities include public cafes, restaurants, lecture hall, outdoor cinemas, and gym. The proposal also integrates the landmark Murr tower and acts as a podium for a number of private high-rises above that will partly fund the new faculty. The typical vertical atrium type found in the educational building is transformed into a differentiated plan and section in order to provide suitable conditions for the varying programme and circulatory requirements and organise the hierarchy of public and private spaces. **3.44** Model view of the faculty building. **3.45** Sectional and plan transformation of

the typical atrium. **3.46** Diagrammatic ground and first floor plan showing the differentiated atrium spaces on each floor level. **3.47** Site plan. **3.48** Longitudinal section. **3.49** Axonometric view.

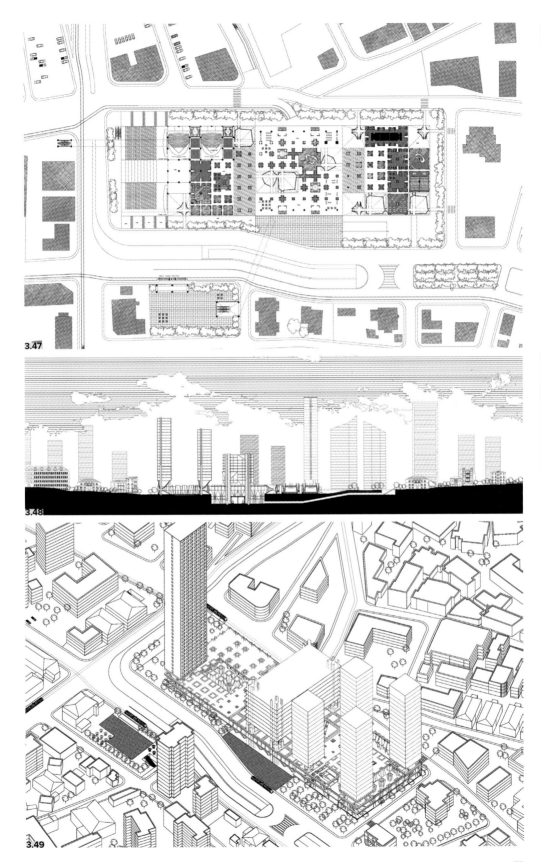

3.47

3.48

3.49

Marseille

Destination and Refuge

Platon Issaias, Camila Sotomayor

Our Cluster initiates a project for Marseille that sees the city through the lens of its historic conditions: destination and refuge. Rather than viewing the city as if it is composed of accidental, informal, spontaneous or neutral forces, we understand Marseille's development as ruled by a series of different stages, which reflect the city's different political, social and cultural statuses. These moments of interruption, of significant change in the city's social consistency, political organisation and territorial reference should be understood as the foundation of Marseille's evolution as a city-refuge, the destination for multitudes of immigrants, workers, forced and voluntary travelers of the Mediterranean and the European mainland. We understand Marseille not as a city within a static territory but a city responsive to the greater politicised space of the Mediterranean. From this point we posit that the city has employed tactics in order to survive inside the dynamic of a larger territory and at the scale of the city and its architecture.

During consecutive waves of immigration and population influxes, the city grew to become the second largest in France, the country's largest and most important port, an extremely significant historic working class centre and one of the most diverse and multicultural cities in Europe. The cluster explores a pedagogical method to investigate and, more importantly, to capture and to render these very dynamic conditions. The cluster's ethos towards Marseille insisted on its performativity as case study that could paradigmatically represent two complementary conditions in various historic moments: the city as an infrastructure of economic and geopolitical dominance, but also as a city with a peculiar autonomy. Through its history, morphology and social structure, Marseille embodies a paradigm of the Mediterranean city and the reasoning behind our agenda:
- The relation of cities with the politics of space
- The expanded concept of territory and sovereignty in the region and its respective

treatment historically until the present
- Population movements – internal and external
- Commerce and trade
- Above all, conflicts and struggles of peoples, collectives and individuals for survival and dominance in the city, the region and the whole Mediterranean Sea.

This final point is of fundamental importance to our project, as we endeavour to avoid a research trajectory that imposes a romantic view on the Mediterranean and its historic urban centres.

Our archaeology for Marseille measures the importance of the city as an urban formation inhabited by traces of both an ancient and a recent past. The premise of the Cluster is to relate Marseille's past and contemporary conditions with the technology of the port and the infrastructure of trade. This constitutes a spatial strategy which uncovers fragments of the city's social and political activity. The operation becomes the foundation upon which our project is built and demands a synthesis of material composed of these fragments: the actual configuration of the city; its history and geology; its infrastructure; and the architectural spaces that represent the subjects shaped within it. The proposals incorporate this almost archaeological knowledge of the city within tactics or protocols that reinforce Marseille's contemporary position as a city that has embraced moments of crisis to become a destination for survivors and exiles. Instead of researching, of 'learning from Marseille', we tried to use the means and the techniques of archaeology, deployed for architecture and urban design. The research is not therefore detached from the essence of the project, but informs our view on the city's existing categorisations, on the patterns of spatial occupation and practices that define a series of architectural archetypes and protocols. We draw, we write and we propose as we investigate the materiality, the actuality, the present and the past of the given reality of Marseille.

In all nine projects of the Cluster, the main points of interest became Marseille's relation to the sea, the port and the historic and contemporary forms of production in the city. It is precisely the expanded territorial significance of Marseille that allows us to think of architectural and urban strategies that could address multiple scales and human practices. From the industrial heritage of the port to the educational complexes and the railway infrastructure, from the traces of the city wall to the contemporary refugee settlements, from the new, environmentally sensitive waterbus infrastructure to the radical reconfiguration of the port, from the monumentality of the proposed piers to the series of 'domestic frames' that colonise the landscape of Marseille, the Cluster investigated possible typologies, spaces not just to accommodate but to radicalise the way the city is experienced and inhabited today.

We would like to thank Ross Exo Adams, Aristide Antonas, William Firebrace, Luca Garofalo, Sam Jacoby, Adrian Lahoud, Godofredo Pereira, Lorenzo Pezzani, Marco Poletto, Charles Rice, Davide Sacconi, Douglas Spencer, Eyal Weisman and Elia Zenghelis.

Students
Petra Bartosova, Fan Chen, Yingnan Chu, Xiaonan Li, Laura Gabrielle Risseeuw, Sheng Yang Zhang, Tian Zhang, Hongmei Zheng, Jiaqi Zheng, Yuan Hong Wang

4.1

4.1 Édouard Baldus, Marseille, Rail Yards of the Marseille
Station, Late 1850s, Metropolitan Museum of Art (detail).
© The Metropolitan Museum of Art/Art Resource/Scala,
Florence **4.2** Marseille, plan of the city's metropolitan area.

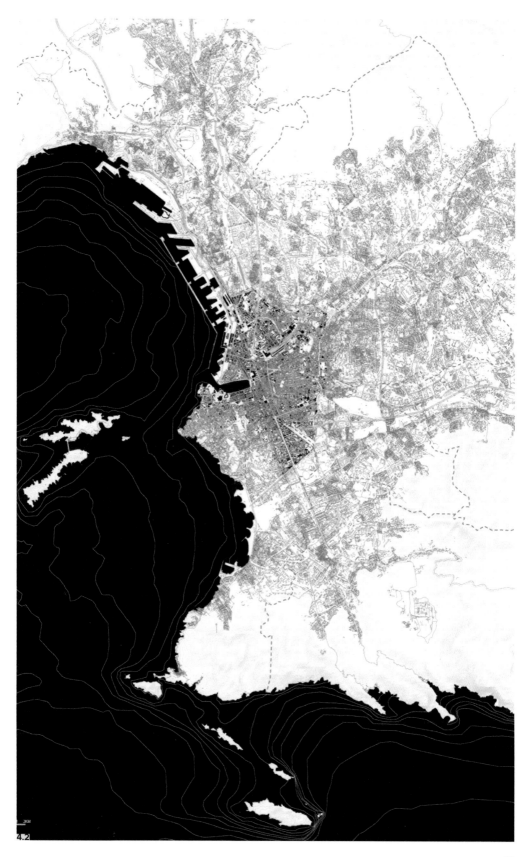

2KM

4.2

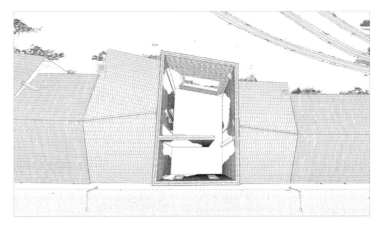

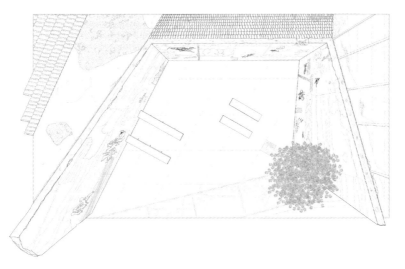

4.3

4.3 **Laura Gabrielle Risseeuw** Site Plan of Ruede Lyon, the Planier Path and the Suffren. The project consists of a network of 36 public spaces throughout Marseille and is influenced by the history and tradition of the conceptual appeal of Marseille in the 19th and 20th centuries. With a soft instrumentality, the project seeks to confront the visitor with industrial infrastructure and materiality, either from a distance or immediately. **4.4 Laura Gabrielle Risseeuw** Site Plan of the Panier Path, Canet and Corniche. The project constructs a series of open-air environments, structures and sites formerly unoccupied that have the potential to be repurposed. The project creates spaces that make an impression on the people (inhabitants and visitors) and specific areas of Marseille with a rather infinitesimal way. These subtle changes to the urban landscape offer a new perspective of the city. The sites are visually connected. There is also a connection in terms of materiality and cohesion of design principles.

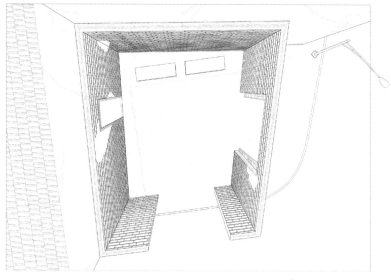

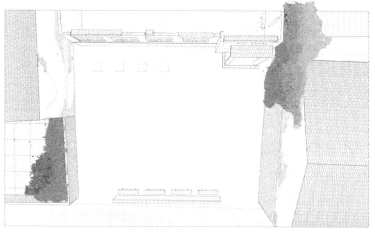

4.4

4.5

4.5 – 4.10 Laura Gabrielle Risseeuw Collage.

4.7

4.8

4.9

4.10

4.11

4.11 Yingnan Chu Domestic Frames. Agricultural Landscape Axonometric. The project uses Marseille as an experimental site to rethink the role of infrastructure in relation to domestic space, in light of the radical transformations of the space of circulation, communication and interaction in the post-Fordist mode of production. This new relationship between productive domestic and infrastructure generates the possibility for a new type of architecture and organisation of forms-of-life. Marseille is analysed as a series of fragmented urban patterns and categorised landscapes. The project focusses on three main environments (post-industrial, agricultural and maritime), investigating the way the domestic sphere is shaped in relation to its surrounding and productive requirements. The proposal frames existing structures, plots and activities, operating as part of the landscape, as a functional machine that organises living and working in the city. The Domestic Frames consist of a proposal, where the different scales of the urban are collapsing in one architectural gesture: from the space of the room and the furniture to the settlement unit and then to a system that colonises territory. The project seeks to produce a new radical view of the role of architecture and urban design in the contemporary city. The prototype of the agricultural site deals with different forms of plants, fruits and products popular in Marseille and the south of France. In the prototype, the technical requirements and the climatic conditions affect the organisation of the interior and the form, the size and the materiality of the units.

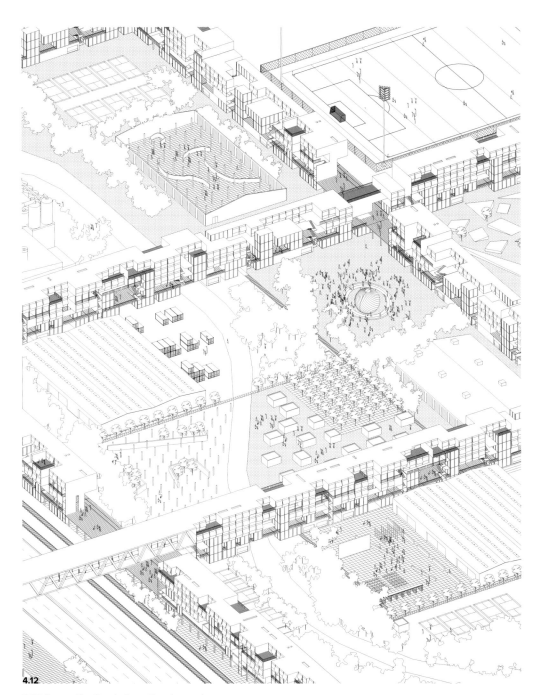

4.12

4.12 Yingnan Chu Post-Industrial Landscape Axonometric.
The post-industrial landscape of Marseille, in most cases the
ruins of the economic decline of the city and its port, becomes
the ideal ground to test the coexistence of different forms of
production and types of domestic organisation. The frames
absorb already existing structures (warehouses, abandoned or
operating factories, manufacturing units, etc), incorporating
them into a unifying circulation network. Public transport
follows the traces of the frame and pedestrians move freely in
the continuous horizontal, ground floor space. The domestic
space collapses within the space of circulation, interaction and
communication. The domestic frame becomes the new
typology for the city, the place to interact and to cooperate
with others.

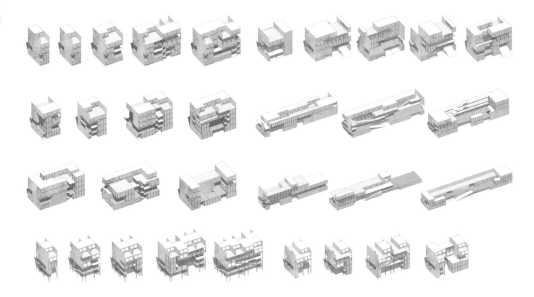

4.13

4.13 – 4.17 Yingnan Chu Domestic Frames **4.13** Details of
post-industrial and agricultural frames. **4.14** Detail of the
agricultural field. **4.15** Detail of the agricultural landscape.
4.16 Detail of the post-industrial landscape.

4.15

4.16

4.17

4.17 Yingnan Chu Interior of the working space.

4.18

4.19

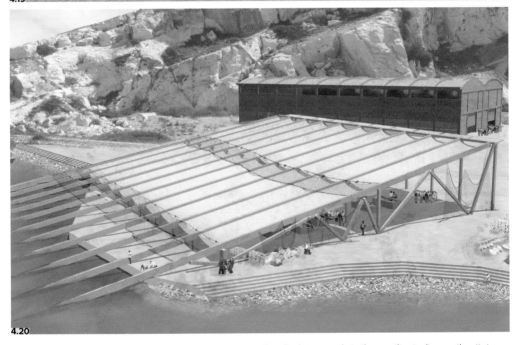

4.20

4.18 – 4.20 Tian Zhang Navigating Marseille: A Waterbus Infrastructure for the City. **4.18** Collage. The project introduces a new public transport system in Marseille, connecting it with the existing transportation networks. The new waterbus brings new life experiences and leisure activities to locals and tourists. In Marseille, the most interesting thing is the beach and the various small ports in the very central area of the city. People can enjoy these sites next to their homes and offices instead of going to suburbs. The intimate relationship with the sea, the beach and the water became the foundation of the project. **4.19** Structural section of the prototypical station. The new waterbus routes are drawn according to the existing ports, marine conditions and environmental requirements and restrictions. These routes not only act as commuting lines but also bring people to the coastline to discover the city in an alternative way. Among the various stops suggested, five sites are selected for further development. Some of them are part of existing routes and the port, and in some other cases the project introduces new possible activities. **4.20** Collage of the station at Frioul Island.

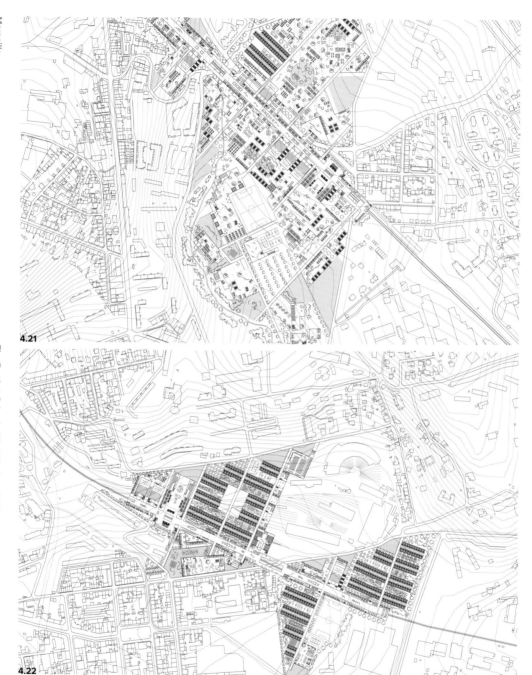

4.21

4.22

4.21 – 4.24 Jiaqi Zheng Cours: Knowledge Crossing. The project proposes the possibility of improving productivity through the mobility of knowledge and the labour force. The aim is to create a new knowledge transportation system by integrating the railway system and reusing vacant industrial lands. The concept of this project is inspired by Cedric Price's Potteries Thinkbelt. The Knowledge Crossing follows this idea and proposes an open campus that can be freely accessed by local communities for various learning, training and producing activities. The Knowledge Crossing would be implemented by the national network of public and adult education centres GRETA (groupement d'établissements) as the infrastructure for residents in regional and national level. **4.21** Learning Centre – Site A. **4.22** Housing Project – Site B. The Knowledge

Crossing is a campus that consists of three facilities located in sites spread along the railway line, from the northwest to the southeast of Marseille. For geographical and historical reasons, the railway follows the direction of urban and industrial expansion, also called the 'spine line'. The Knowledge Crossing operates as not only a campus, but also is a transportation spine traversing the communities it serves, rather than building a single concentrated location. These three sites have different functions but are tightly connected through rail and the educational activities. **4.23** Learning Centre – Site A. **4.24** Housing Project – Site B.

4.23

4.24

4.25 **Jiaqi Zheng** Cours: Knowledge Crossing. Campus Scenes.

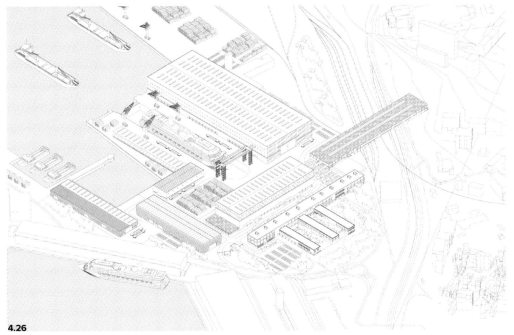

4.26

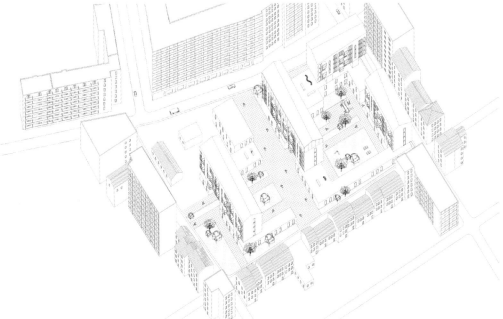

4.27

4.26 Fan Chen Workshops and Factories: Beyond the
Euroméditerranée and towards an alternative strategy for
Marseille's Port. Axonometric. The project selects and analyses
three different types of urban spaces in the port area of
Marseille. Different densities, architectural forms, productive
facilities and housing typologies are proposed according to
the particular requirements of the three neighborhood units.
In each case, a central spine and a series of open, public
spaces unite the small-scale fragments. **4.27 Petra Bartosova**
Vieille Charité Saint Charles. Axonometric. The project
introduces five complexes in Marseille that provide housing
to immigrants and low-income households. It also suggests
a radical modification of the existing immigration policies in
France and the Mediterranean.

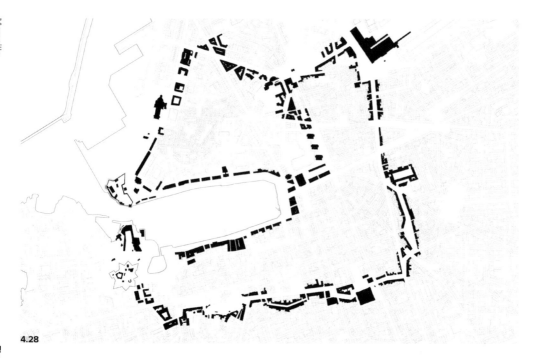

4.28

4.29

4.30

4.28 Xiaonan Li, Hongmei Zheng The Wall. The project consists of a systematic investigation of the city's defensive wall, in an effort to trace it back to Marseille. The team argues that the transformation of the wall was always indicating the way the city is conveyed. The project, by absorbing boulevards and streets into one unifying system, introduces again the thickness of the wall, which can be considered a political infrastructure, a new spatial apparatus that identifies fields of relation. The discrete pieces of space, the episodes of the new path are incorporated through a dynamic process of articulation, cooperation as well as division. **4.29 Shengyang Zhang** Port machinery: The 3 piers **4.30 Shengyang Zhang** View of cargo harbour from container ship. **4.31 Xiaonan Li, Hongmei Zheng** The Wall. Collage, detail of Boulevard d'Athènes from the monumental staircase of Gare Saint Charles.

4.31

Messina
and Reggio
Calabria

South to South: Excursions on the Border of the Mediterranean

Luca Galofaro, Davide Sacconi

The Mediterranean is a huge liquid boundary that divides and at the same time connects territories. It maintains differences and at the same time attempts to keep them together.[1] At the centre of the Mediterranean the imaginary line that divides north and south materialises in a few kilometers of salt water, a geographical border that separates Africa and Europe, the Italian peninsula (extreme southern Europe) and the island of Sicily (extreme north Africa).

For millennia this edge has been a place of exchange and commerce, a theatre of encounters and clashes of different peoples and diverse cultures. But at the same time it is a place of people clustered in groups of isolated towns and villages, sometimes remote and inaccessible, where rituals are repeated and customs preserved throughout time. Two faces of the same coin: the unstable and dynamic innovation brought by the sea and the archaic tradition of the society rooted in the landscape.

Openness and isolation, agriculture and neglected spaces, care and abandonment, landscape and urbanisation, are the constituent elements of a structural duality, a physical and conceptual territory to be deciphered in all its implication exploring and analysing the thin limit that divides legality and illegality, wild exploitation of resources and the formation of a peculiar political subjectivity.

Such a duality is epitomised by the lifelong conflict between Messina and Reggio Calabria, a theoretical city constituted by two facing urban constellations separated by a sea inlet, a geographical limit that metaphorically embodies the border as the fundamental condition of the Mediterranean Sea. The coastlines of Messina and Reggio Calabria are today part of a vast territorial network, where an 'urban powder' blown over an exceptional natural scenery, throughout carefully cultivated land and large abandoned industrial areas, is bound together by infrastructural, cultural and economic interests.

A place here and now, where the urban fabric has lost its formal structure to become a mere infrastructure for information, relations, services and commodities.

The architectural scale is here directly confronted with the territorial scale without any possible mediation of planning and economic management techniques. From this perspective such a peculiar condition is the ideal environment where architecture as project for the city is called to revert the paradigm of the south. Rather than be conceived as a problem of underdevelopment in respect to the north the south embodies the possibility of an alternative model for social, political, and economical development. Confronted with the dissolution of the Socialist experiment and the crisis of international Capitalism, we claim the south as a resource of human energy, memories and relationships, as a possibility for a different ethos of Europe within a global world.

Architecture as Urban Design
The object of the Cluster research is the relationship between architecture and city, a link that is disappearing from contemporary architectural theory and practice, flattened between the run for seductive images and iconic buildings, the immediacy of urban activism and the complexity of data management for a fluid and unlimited urbanisation.

But if on one side architecture today is mostly reduced to a fashionable product, to an aesthetic commodity subjected to the existing conditions, on the other side it can still be considered in its autonomy, as form in relationship with the territory. In contrast to the smooth, fast and isotropic character of urbanisation, architecture is finite, slow and clumsy. Its peculiar attribute is to record the memories, the conflicts, the beauty and the harshness of our environment within a specific form. Working with discontinuities and accepting conflicts as a vital aspect of urban life, architecture can still offer critical resistance to current practices of urbanisation, and claim the right to elaborate and test alternative paradigms for the city.

The work of the Cluster is as an experimental attempt of considering architecture not as a consequence of masterplanning but as a primary tool for urban design. Rather than propose mere design, a management tool of the urban conflicts, the projects aim for an architecture that can expose the complexity and contradictions of the territory and therefore foster political awareness through physical transformation.

The projects tackled a variety of complex issues that dramatically affect urban life linking it to the specific form of urbanisation of the Messina Strait territory and to a wider history of Italy within the European and the Mediterranean context. The juridical state of exception of illegal immigrants is juxtaposed with the extra-territorial legal status of the international Gioia Tauro harbour (Constantinos Marcou). The tradition of agriculture as a resource is opposed to the current neglect of the productive landscape (Valeria Piras). The terrific beauty of the unique coastline faces the abandonment of industrial production (Steve Revill). The dramatic encounter between the man-made grid structure of the city, following the earthquake destruction, and the irreducible power of the natural landscape (Boaz Rotem and Diego Vergara). The rigid block structure of the grid as an opportunity to rethink the boundaries between legal and illegal buildings, private and public domain (Christina Varvogli and Aglaia Kornilia Tsolakidis).

Through the historical and archeological reconstruction of the overlapping layers of infrastructure, urbanisation and landscape, the projects unfolded the material conditions of the area as problematisation: 'the development of a domain of acts, practices, and thoughts that pose problems'.[2] Rather than thinking architecture in terms of concepts or functions, the projects expose a palimpsest of issues and possibilities through the definition of architectural form in relationship with the territory.

We would like to thank our guest critics:
Pier Vittorio Aureli, Andrea Bagnato, Alberto Iacovoni, Gabriele Mastrigli, Ivonne Santoyo Orozco, Lorenzao Pezzani, Francesco Sebregondi, Elia Zenghelis.

Students
Mercedes Araya Garcia, Jialong Chai, Yuhuan Kong, Jing Liu, Constantinos Marcou, Marie Park, Li Pi, Valeria Piras, Stephen Revill, Boaz Rotem, Theodora Soulonia, Yang Sun, Yan Tai, Aglaia Tsolakidi, Christina Varvogli, Diego Jose Vergara, Junjie Wang, Jia You Wei.

1. Franco Cassano, *Homo Civicus*, Edizioni Dedalo, Bari, 2004, p.108.
2. Michel Foucault, *Polemics, Politics and Problematizations*, interview by Paul Rabinow – 1984, in "Essential Works of Foucault", volume 1 "Ethics", The New Press, 1997.

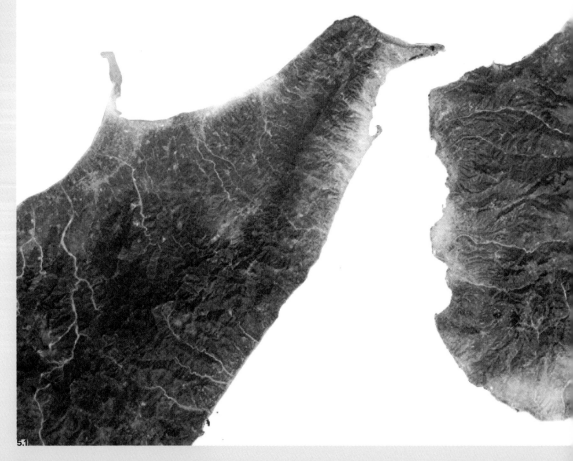

5.1

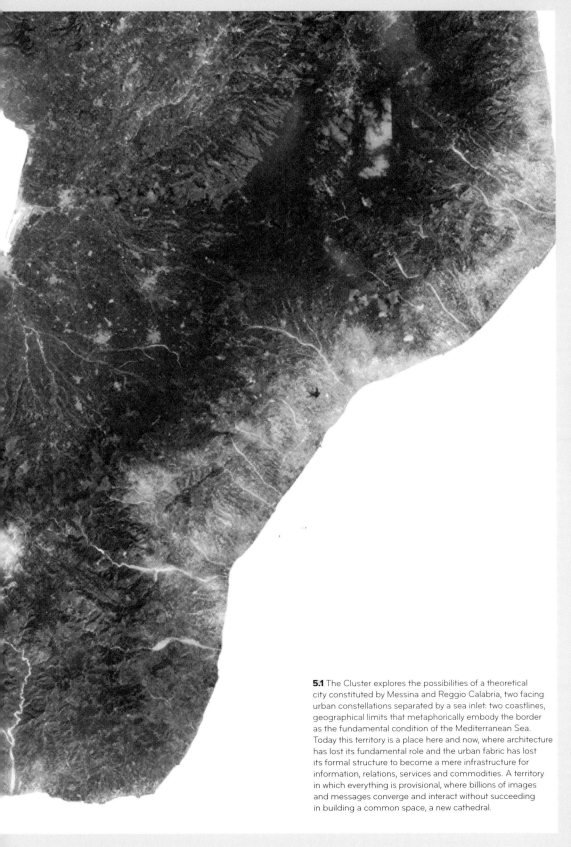

5.1 The Cluster explores the possibilities of a theoretical city constituted by Messina and Reggio Calabria, two facing urban constellations separated by a sea inlet: two coastlines, geographical limits that metaphorically embody the border as the fundamental condition of the Mediterranean Sea. Today this territory is a place here and now, where architecture has lost its fundamental role and the urban fabric has lost its formal structure to become a mere infrastructure for information, relations, services and commodities. A territory in which everything is provisional, where billions of images and messages converge and interact without succeeding in building a common space, a new cathedral.

5.2

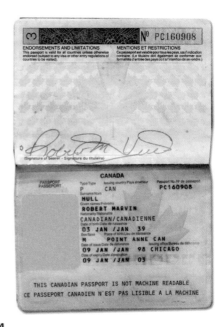

5.3

5.4

5.5

5.2 – 5.4 Constantinos Marcou The Mediterranean as a System of Invisible Thresholds. The multiplicity of cultural and geopolitical conditions at the Mediterranean scale create invisible lines that affect the understanding of this territory as highly fragmented, divided into smaller pieces. This body of water has often been romanticised through the idea of the sea as a border and as a connecting element. Instead the studying of the complex maritime jurisdiction, the configuration of 'territorial' seas, the establishment of exclusive economic zones and specific traffic roots and transportation protocols, opens up another reading of this platform. The sea acquires a spatial and physical dimension: a space that is not neutral anymore, but it is rather a reflection of its complex network of boundaries, of mechanisms of control that aim to exclude any unwanted or unexpected trespassing, redefining the idea of the Mediterranean as a system of invisible thresholds.

5.5 Constantinos Marcou The State of Exception and the Domestic Life. The system of invisible thresholds are forcing the limits between state control and legitimacy, human rights and the concept of domestic life. In this example an Egyptian man travelled from Cairo to Gioia Tauro holding a fake Canadian passport: he was locked inside a shipping container which he transformed into a home for his long journey.

5.6 – 5.7 Constantinos Marcou From 'Bare Life' to Threshold of Knowledge. The project departs from a speculation around the extra-territorial character of Gioia Tauro both as one of the largest containership harbour's of the Mediterranean and as the location of one of the Italian identification and detention

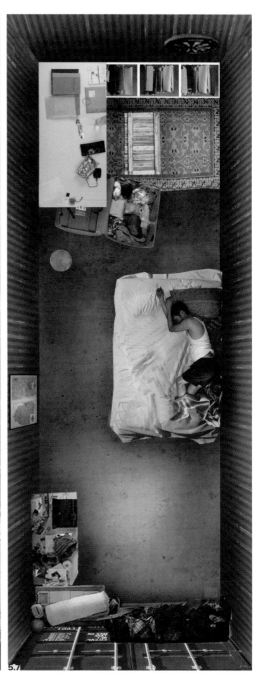

5.6

5.7

centres for illegal immigrants, as well as a place where immigrants are exploited and reduced to bare life conditions by criminal organisations that control the flourishing agricultural production. The aim is to enforce the 'liminal' character of the space constructing a system of thresholds to liberate the 'otherness' through knowledge. The project materialises in a platform based on the common space, where the encounter between local inhabitants and migrant can produce a social and political substance manifested in space. The idea of threshold refers to the possibility to create spatial in between conditions that could lead to a reconfiguration of the political and social configuration of the territory. The 'camp' can therefore be reconsidered not as a secluded enclave but rather as a window of unexpected opportunities in between the

hyper controlled space of flows. Thresholds of knowledge manifest itself as a sanctuary, a neutral territory that politically belongs only to those who inhabit it.

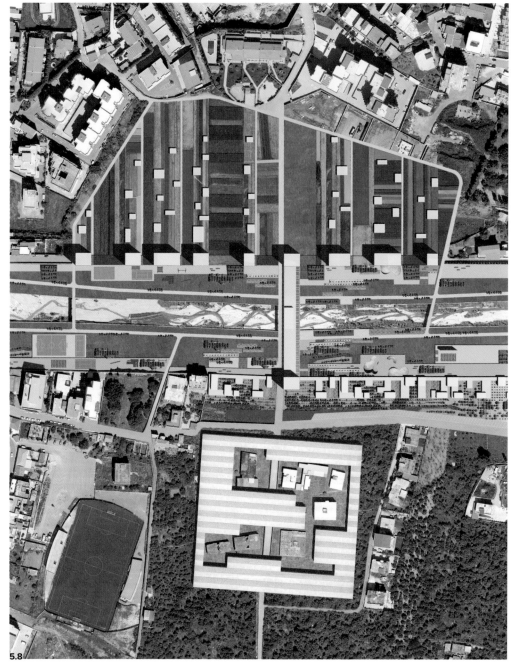

5.8

5.8 Valeria Piras From Abandoned Landscape to Landscape of Production. The territory of Reggio Calabria is the result of a continuous process of destruction and reconstruction, where the chaotic overlapping and juxtaposition of different layers, together with the social and political structure, has generated the conditions for the actual landscape of abandonment. The small streams called Fiumara, dry for most part of the year and are characterised by a violent flow of water during winter, constitute the main natural structure of such a landscape. At the same time the wall can be recognised as the architectural element that characterises this neglected landscape, working both as a device that divides and constitutes the infrastructure of the territory, but also as the element that protects the landscape from urbanisation.

The project elaborates a strategy of intervention starting from the rethinking of the wall as as the structural element of an alternative territorial configuration, where the abandoned agricultural landscape is dialectically confronting the urban fabric, redefining the limits of urbanisation. The aim is to generate a political and economical space not creating smooth connections but rather defining a territorial system through the interaction of different forms of production: leisure (the park along the river), knowledge (the agricultural school that connects the two sides), cultivated lands and productive facilities (greenhouse) and housing (defining the new borders along the river).

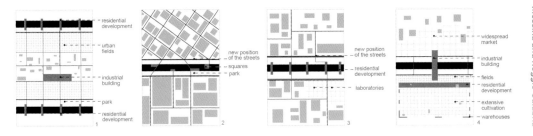

5.9

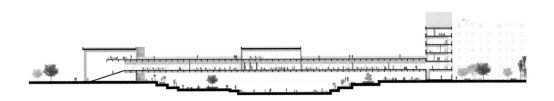

5.10

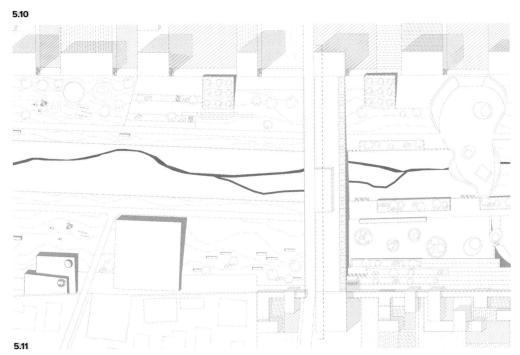

5.11

5.9 Valeria Piras Strategic Principles of Intervention. Acknowledging of the impossibility for the city of Reggio Calabria to generate a economic critical mass that could lead to the extensive recovering of the abandoned landscape of the Fiumaras, the project chooses to focus on the definition of strategic principles rather than proposing a comprehensive masterplan. The strategy defines the elements and the protocols through which the production could be reactivated step by step in different areas along the rivers, dialectically responding to the diversity of the existing conditions. The mix of different forms of production (leisure, knowledge, cultivated lands, productive facilities and housing), organised through a system of walls, is the constant element: all the projects work as machines that will develop over time transforming the city in

a field of production. **5.10 – 5.11 Valeria Piras** The Wall as Landscape Structure. The Fiumara stream is redefined as a productive territory through a system of walls that explicitly expose its limits both as protective elements from the seasonal overflowing and as boundaries of the urbanisation. The wall, unpacking in a series of parallel lines, defines a sequence of terraces and paths that organise an artificial landscape that could host different uses in different periods of the year, according to the water flow. The university will be the element that physically connects the two parts of the city facilitating the production of knowledge.

5.12 – 5.13 Valeria Piras The Wall as Limit. The main wall on both sides of the Fiumara has been re-imagined according to the different character of the city fabric that it is confronted with, giving a different form in both sides to a new residential development. The southern edge, being located in a part of the city that it is not yet urbanised, is designed as a compact closure and a strong boundary, exposing the harsh contrast between the landscape of production and the city. Conversely on the north side of the Fiumara the wall becomes a fragmented system that separates the river from the city, where the definition of the limit is assured by rhythmic alternation of residential towers and the redesign of the embankment of the river. These towers are conceived as a strong presence that will clearly define the limit of the city.

5.14

5.14 Stephen Revill Restructuring the Productive Landscape. The region of Messina and Reggio Calabria is characterised by a contrast between care and neglect: a traditional care of the landscape, embodied in millennia of sophisticated agricultural practices, juxtaposed with the large-scale abandonment of industrial areas, developed through State interventions and under the speculation of European Union funds. The project addresses the post-industrial landscape of the South, using as a case study the San Ranieri Peninsula in the city of Messina. After an archaeological reading and reconstruction of the elements that constitute the physical structure of the context, the project proposes a restructuring of the productive landscape through the systematic use of the wall as the spatial and urban device.

The proposed integration and juxtaposition of spaces for manufacturing, artisan industries, education, culture and leisure as modes of production attempts to reconsider the way in which post-industrial landscapes are conventionally construed. Utilising an architecture of emptiness, developed through a striped organisation of space, the intervention refrains from prescribing overbearing programmes that would inevitably destroy the rich complexity of the site. Instead, the severe logic of the intervention, operating in contrast with the chaotic overlapping of the existing structures, unlocks the potential of the existing structures within a coherent spatial framework. The readability of the landscape orientated around a new layer of circulation will allow multiplicity of uses and practices of re-appropriation, to populate the area.

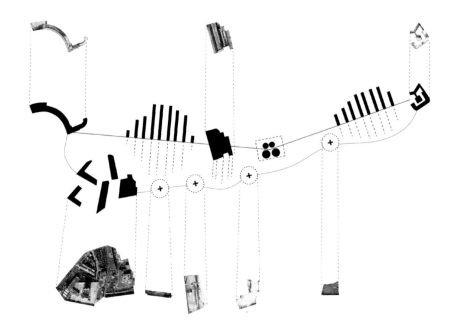

5.15

5.16

5.17

5.18

5.19

5.15 Stephen Revill Restructuring the Productive Landscape. The landscape is a complex and contrasting combination of the natural and the built environments that exist on the San Ranieri Peninsula. The rich materiality that defines existing elements is explored as a means through which the open spaces can be orchestrated as a series of differing and complementary experiences in order to integrate the interventions with the existing spaces and buildings. This allows a restructuring of the territory through interventions that operate upon three main principles: the wall as spatial structure, re-use of existing structures, and connectivity. A pedestrianised spine is inserted through the centre of the site connecting the area to the city whilst tying the elements together along a linear path. This is supplemented by a

treatment of the landscape through a logic that rejects the former stratification of the area, maximising permeability. **5.16 – 5.19 Stephen Revill** Connectivity as Landscape Integration. By imposing a new layer of pedestrian connectivity, existing spaces are revealed and co-ordinated, taking on new purpose whilst respecting archaeological and industrial heritage and memories. Autonomy and possibility are embraced through the merger of juxtaposing functions whilst engaging with existing elements of the landscape to give new purpose and defining new amenities for the wider region as a network of public space is unravelled, integrating the San Ranieri peninsula with the immediate hinterland.

5.20

5.21

5.20 – 5.21 Stephen Revill The Wall as Territorial Structure. The insertion of the wall as the elementary architectural element restructures the productive landscape and provides the permanent foundations of a flexible growth structure. The volume of the walls represent their capacity to restructure the territory whilst their emptiness and the open-ended nature of the striped organisation exposes the potential, and embraces the possibility, of reappropriation by the user. The stark juxtaposition in materiality between the productive space of the ground floor and the residential units expresses the ability of the structure to adapt to demand, providing access to a low-cost live/work arrangement. The structures are arranged to enable a hierarchy of streets with varying frontages whilst the end units provide space for commercial and civic functions that animate the central spine to which the elements are attached.

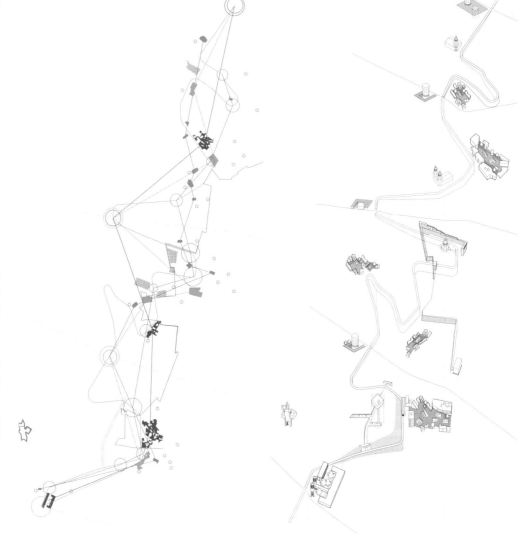

5.22

5.22 – 5.23 Boaz Rotem, Diego Jose Vergara. A Procession between Landscape and Urbanisation. In the city of Messina, the relationship between the landscape and the city can be traced along a single line, a street. By following the topography, this winding road draws the history of the city. Symbolically, it follows the old limit of the city, the walls, and it still holds the symbolical relationship between the urban and the natural through the different layers of its rich history. As such, it houses a unique agglomeration of urban artefacts, conditions, ruins, opening and views, which express the historical strata which has been preserved in this fault between the city and landscape. Today, this road is deprived of its functional use as a main transportation route, a condition that enables to emphasise its symbolic role in the city. The proposal

5.23

for Messina consists of a series of projects along this line. By that it evokes an idea of a procession – a necklace of architectural interventions, which set the rhythm and character of the circulation as an attempt to resist the imposed rational urban structure and to introduce a different way of life. Thus the street becomes a stage for public performance, a venue to enjoy time and space, communal activity and leisure. Therefore, using simple architectural operations, the projects set out to prepare the ground for future activity, emphasising what is already there while keeping the empty vacancy, rather than trying to fill the voids.

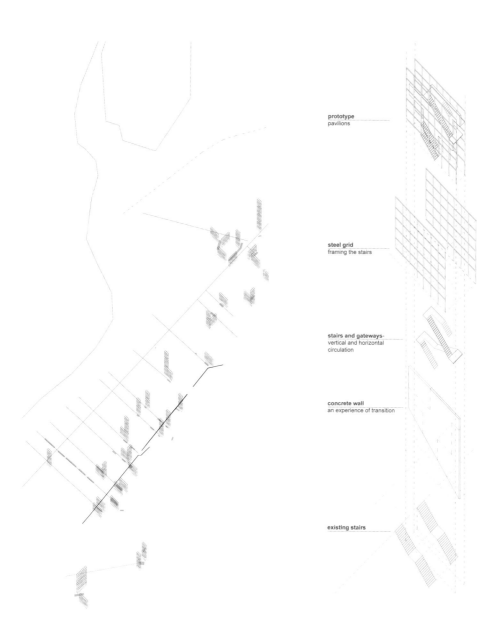

prototype
pavilions

steel grid
framing the stairs

stairs and gateways-
vertical and horizontal
circulation

concrete wall
an experience of transition

existing stairs

5.24

5.25

5.24 – 5.25 Boaz Rotem, Diego Jose Vergara A Celebration between Landscape and Urbanisation. While in Messina the relationship between the city and landscape is drawn by a line, in Reggio Calabria this edge condition is managed through the city structure: a cloud of stairways express the fault – the urban condition where the city's imposed structure is confronted by the landscape. The stairs are the most banal way in which the grid manages topography. This spatial condition is pointed out by the activity of ascending or descending. In Reggio Calabria, this activity becomes the essence of the urban experience and a tool to frame and isolate this contradictory relationship. The proposal for Reggio Calabria, sets out exposing these episodic moments as celebration of the urban fault – by ascending or descending, giving it a distinct architectural form. The interventions propose tools to exaggerate the stairs, making them redundant in order to alienate them from their context, transforming them in an instrument through which one can get a glimpse of the essential character of the city. Every stairway becomes a pavilion, a part of distinct and recognisable architectural elements which perform as stages where people can engage both with the city and the landscape in a collective theatrical act. The pavilions incorporate a single architectural language, thus linking the scale of the basic detail of the pavilion assembly instructions to that of the urban structure.

5.26

5.27

5.28

5.29

5.30

5.31

5.26 – 5.31 Boaz Rotem, Diego Jose Vergara Stairs Flooding. A continual history of destruction resulting from earthquakes and WW2 has left vacant pockets along the road. These voids in the city structure contain bits of ruins which commemorate the traumatic history of Messina. The project frames these conditions in the city by washing these areas with an abstract background of stairs, leaving the ruins as pavilions for future activity. **5.28 Boaz Rotem, Diego Jose Vergara** Inside the Landscape. Perhaps the strongest engagement of the city with the landscape is expressed in this underground tunnel – an abandoned piece of infrastructure which used to connect two parts of the city through the mountain. It is where the city enters the landscape and the landscape has its effect on the city. The project suggests using the tunnel as a link between the level of the city and the level of the road on the topography. **5.29 – 5.31 Boaz Rotem, Diego Jose Vergara** City Walls. The road traces approximately the route of the old city wall, the ancient limit which was partly destroyed during the earthquake of 1908. The project reinterprets the survived segments of the old wall and points out a possible link between them as a symbolic linear way of experiencing the city. The link between the segments is provided by bridges, staircases and empty spaces, offering the possibility to engage both with the tactile experience of the heavy wall and with the Messina Strait landscape, exposed through selected panoramic view over the city.

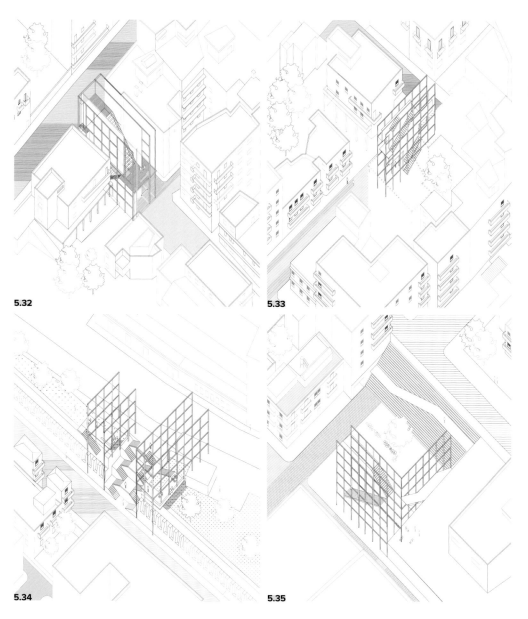

5.32

5.33

5.34

5.35

5.32 – 5.35 Boaz Rotem, Diego Jose Vergara Stairs as Strategic Protocol. The projects in Reggio Calabria perform as tools that adjust to their specific locations. Each pavilion is replacing an urban stairway and extends the experience of ascending and descending, emphasising by means of space and time the exact point in which the over-imposed grid clashes against the steepness of the natural landscape. The specificity of each pavilion is drawn from an analysis that defined different typologies of interventions according to the specificities of esach location: an intervention which is an extension of a street, an intervention on a wall, an intervention on a square, or an open space. The project is therefore conceived as a strategic protocol of intervention that could potentially extend over the entire city as a recognisable element, while at the same time each singular episode unfolds a site-specific project. The project therefore aims to reveal the common and fundamental essence of the city, offering at the same time the ground for a spontaneous reappropriation.

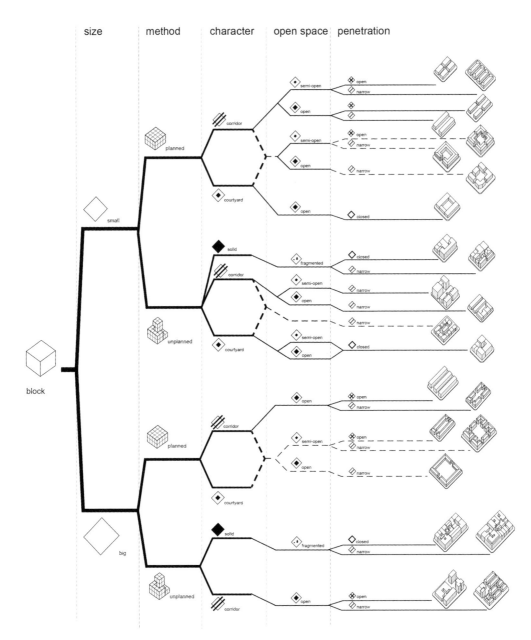

size method character open space penetration

5.36

5.36 Aglaia Tsolakidi, Christina Varvogli Genealogy of the Urban Block. The history of Messina and Reggio Calabria constitute a quite exceptional case in the panorama of Italian cities, since the traces of their urban history have been repeatedly erased by the violence of earthquakes and wars. Therefore other than the natural landscape, the two cities share, at least in the central areas, the grid as a tool for reconstruction and organisation of the city. The project departs from a reading of the two cities as constituted by blocks. The block is understood as a unit, a basic element of the city structure which, through its morphological and material characteristics, provides a specific form of organisation within the circulation the framework set out by the grid. The characteristics of the blocks in Messina and Reggio

Calabria are genealogically reconstructed through a classification that is based on three basic block categories: solid blocks, blocks with a corridor and blocks with a courtyard. The variation of these basic factors shape the different spatial relationship that occur in the urban space in both cities setting out the block as the fundamental element through which the city structure can be understood, interpreted and manipulated.

5.37 – 5.38 Aglaia Tsolakidi, Cristina Varvogli The Grid: The Potential of the Common. The grid is an organisation principle that can be read both as an abstract principle and as well as the very material form. The project sets out from the idea of exposing the material consequences of the grid, its unrivalled power of the management of city life. The city can be conceived and represented as a three-dimensional grid of possibilities. The existing city, in its material form, is just one of the possible outcomes that emerge out of the same specific declination of such an organisational system. Exposing the potential the project aims to make explicit the possibilities of transformation that is inherent to the grid principle emphasising the precarious and the same time absolute character of the grid. From this perspective the blocks can be read as something more than just parts of the city grid, as they represent a unit of spatial organisation that has distinct borders. The block can be understood as an intermediate level of urban space between the public and the private, and as a unit it can provide a level of autonomy. The project proposes a strategy of manipulation of the block through adding and cutting pieces of the grid, which can also lead to linking the created spaces. This strategy suggests the redesign of the relationship between public, private and common spaces on a block's level with an emphasis on common spaces. These transformations aim to provide spatial qualities that could shape a new political awareness and a collective subjectivity, establishing the block as fundamental unit of the city as well as the basic social and political institution.

5.39

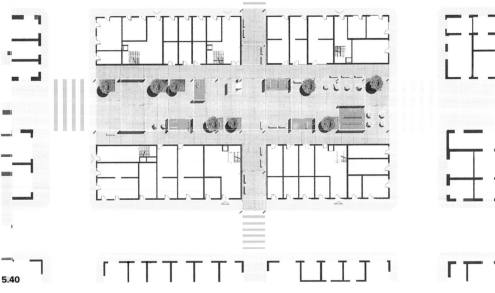

5.40

5.39 – 5.40 Aglaia Tsolakidi, Cristina Varvogli Urban Shelter. By simple means of cutting and adding, the liberated space of the block reveals its large range of potentialities. The linear in-between space of the block can become an open corridor, a passage, creating a space with different levels of privacy and publicness. The qualities and the level of opening to the public of the common space can be negotiated within the block community ranging from a close courtyard to an open link offered to the neighbourhood. The opening of the corridor can potentially lead to the linking of the block's space with the city, revealing that the simple manipulation of the space of the block has the potential to extend at the level of the entire city. The adding is applied by framing the created space and the possibilities for social interaction and movement. From this perspective, architecture, rather than being conceived as design, as a management tool for urbanisation, acquires a paradigmatic value, opening up the possibility of a different project for the city.

5.42 Aglaia Tsolakidi, Cristina Varvogli Pavilion of the Common. The variation in block typologies and the flexibility of the grid allow it to implement different variations on each block highlighting the block's basic character. In the case of a block with corridors and a courtyard, a pavilion for common spaces is added in order to reformulate the relationship between private inner-side of the block and the public level of the street. The choice of elevating the common level on pilotis suggests the possibilities of a more complex declination of the relationship between public and private space: the courtyard of the block has the possibility of gaining a public character, by using the existing corridors that provide access to the inner space.
5.43 – 5.44 Aglaia Tsolakidi, Cristina Varvogli Common Frame. The in-between space of an existing block with a corridor can be freed and gain a public character. The basic element of the block, the corridor, is highlighted and it is used in order to create a link, a passage. The common spaces are again provided on a different level form the ground, on top of the existing buildings. Part of the terrace is used to organise a line of residential spaces: the alternation between common and private spaces in the organisation of the housing as a check board exposes and materialises the filled and empty rhythm of the three-dimensional grid. The similarity of the façade and the plan view allow a simple understanding of organisation that can be suggested for the self-organisation of people and autonomy.

Tangier

6

Tangier
Contestation / Collaboration

Peter Besley, Hannah Corlett, Jonathan Kendall

We are interested in how the city can be understood as a field of stakes and protagonists, rather than the conventional conception as a grouping of disinterested objects revealed in mapping. This stance posits that meaning in the urban environment arises from use and is not latent in objects. We are therefore interested in the mechanisms through which resources are used within the city via processes of contestation and collaboration.

The Cluster's geographical focus is the Mediterranean coastal region of northern Morocco. The Tangier-Tetouan area can be seen as a microcosm of phenomena that operate at multiple scales across the Mediterranean. At the same time, it represents a distinctive condition shaped by its geographical position and historic processes of colonisation and migratory flows. The city sits in a strategic location between Africa and Europe, between the Atlantic Ocean and the Mediterranean Sea. Tangier is also shaped by multiple boundary conditions, nested within one another, overlapping and adjacent. These have historically defined its strategic value and continue to shape its contemporary condition.

Tangier has been a colonial outpost, an International Zone, and is today the northernmost region of the monarchical Moroccan state. The region is currently undergoing rapid development, with investments including construction of a European-funded Free Zone, a new container port, new towns and related high-speed rail and road networks. As a consequence of these moves, and the rapid pace of internal migration, the population has trebled in the last 30 years.

In this context, the region can be seen as a territory exemplifying contestation and collaboration in its distribution of spatial, economic and social resources. Tangier operates within and beyond multiple boundaries. Disputed territories define its relationship to sovereign neighbours. Economic internal boundaries create taxation advantages in relation to global trading markets. Rapid urbanisation has resulted in the formation of peripheral suburban settlements that blur the boundaries between city and landscape. Through an understanding of the internal and external dynamics that are shaping the transformation of the city, the Cluster aims to propose mechanisms for intervention, which are capable of functioning amongst these complex forces. Central to this is how the city is conceptualised at the outset, which in turn defines the designer's own critical scope and means of operation.

We would like to thank all those who have supported the Cluster during the year, providing advice and direction, as visiting critics and during our visit to Morocco, which was an incredibly formative experience for us all: Medine Altiok, Morad Ameziane, Abdellatif Brini, Eddy Declerc, Aref Hassani, Rachid Houari, Mohamed Jallal, Hicham Kersit, El Moumni Lahbib, Johnny Ojeil, Carlos Perez Marin, Andrew Porter and Abigail Ashton, Hassan Salmi M'Rabet and Elia Zenghelis.

Students
Young Joon Chung, Nithita Fongtanakit, Iulia Fratila, Jiaoyang Fu, Chung-Shing Huang, Shengwen Huang, Yingwen Ke, Heng Liu, Annick Meiers, Nicole Rochette, Nina Vidic Ivancic, Hui Xu, Ching Wei Yang, Hua Zhu

Hui Xu, visualisation from inside a souk

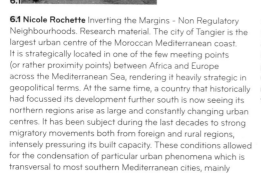

6.1

6.1 Nicole Rochette Inverting the Margins - Non Regulatory Neighbourhoods. Research material. The city of Tangier is the largest urban centre of the Moroccan Mediterranean coast. It is strategically located in one of the few meeting points (or rather proximity points) between Africa and Europe across the Mediterranean Sea, rendering it heavily strategic in geopolitical terms. At the same time, a country that historically had focussed its development further south is now seeing its northern regions arise as large and constantly changing urban centres. It has been subject during the last decades to strong migratory movements both from foreign and rural regions, intensely pressuring its built capacity. These conditions allowed for the condensation of particular urban phenomena which is transversal to most southern Mediterranean cities, mainly

regarding the issue of housing large quantities of new urban populations. This issue has been dealt with differently according to the diverse contexts it is confronted with, and in the case of Tangier, the political conditions favoured a vast proliferation of self-built houses extending the limits of the urban realm. The proposed interventions aim to introduce a new component into the equation: flat open surfaces that will facilitate community activities.

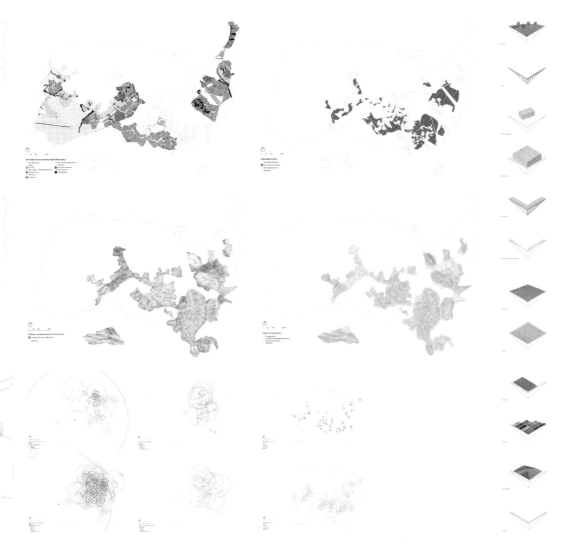

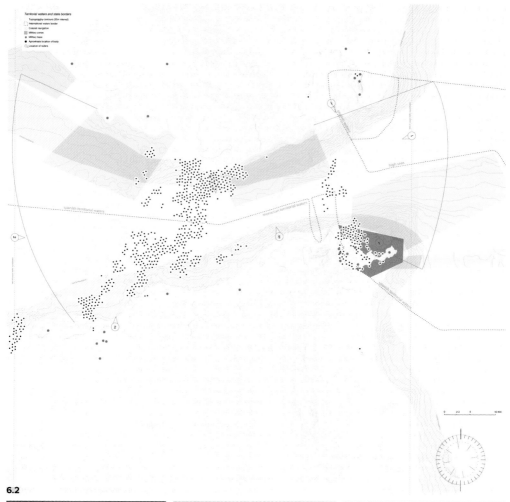

6.2

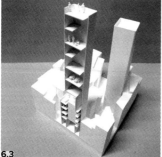

6.3

6.2 – 6.5 Iulia Fratila Overlapping Territories – Tangible Borders. **6.2** Mapping of migration across the Gibraltar Strait. **6.3** Modelling of exchange towers for migrants. Every year, thousands of 'irregulars' die trying to cross the Strait of Gibraltar. Every day, 30,000 Moroccans cross the borders of Ceuta to 'offer' themselves as cleaners, traders, smugglers. Much like other areas in Africa, this is a country which still struggles with poverty. The '97 Declaration of Barcelona brings up a new tool for fighting the root causes of migration to the North i.e. the establishment of free-trade zones in the South. As an immediate effect, we see the apparition of the Ceuta fence in 1998 and the 'electronic wall' along the coastline as predictions of the many special economic zones that have been set up in the past years in the Tangier – Tetouan area.

6.4 Mapping of the market free zone. **6.5** Modelling of the free zone market in this context of increasing social inequality and militarisation of borders, this project starts by questioning the city's relationship with its forbidden hinterland and how it relates to the far territories, and asks, can this spatial binary between Morocco and Spain be reversed? The proposal acknowledges the Moroccan government's plan of building a new commercial free zone near the border to Ceuta and tries to shape it into an instrument for social development, not only economic growth. The project proposes scenarios in which this exceptional space (juridical and economical) could feed the traditional space of a street market.

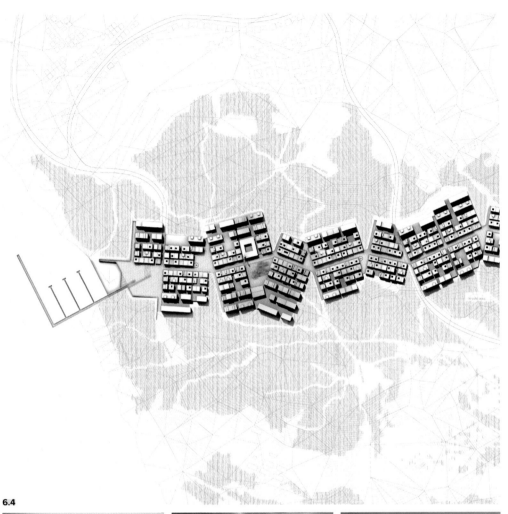

6.4

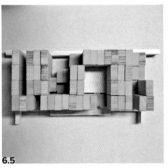

6.5

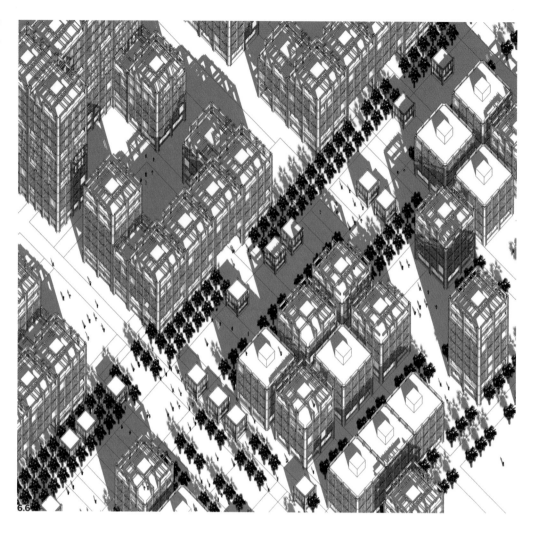

6.6

6.7

6.6 – 6.7 Heng Liu Employment Fostering Zone. The project proposes the introduction of science-based industry to the eastern part of the city. By creating a series of departments, chronographic, according to the location and context, the project creates a big platform, strengthening cooperation between enterprise and research. The target of the project is to foster new types of business among highly educated people, and create new modes of enterprises to balance the 'dependent' economy (on foreign trade and service). The proposal is organised along a linear landscaped campus to serve the local people, functioning as an important spine for the sustainable urban development of the region. **6.6** View of the proposed campus. **6.7** Seven Individual block types.

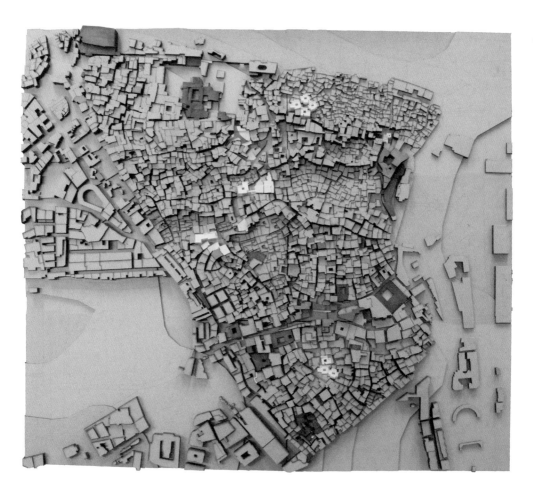

6.8

6.9

6.8 – 6.9 Yingwen Ke Medina Routes System. **6.8** Physical model of the Medina. **6.9** Physical models of proposed new market and housing within the Medina and map of the proposed routes and interventions. By proposing vertical routes linking historic landmarks and newly inserted structures within the Medina, including daily infrastructures, tourism facilities and interweaving social spaces, the project aims to seek a balance between the modernisation and preservation, protecting daily life while gaining benefit from increases in tourism. By containing tourist activities on the routes system, instead of wondering and getting lost in the Medina, tourists would not miss either the legacies or the local life in the Medina while natives could have both privacy and economic opportunity.

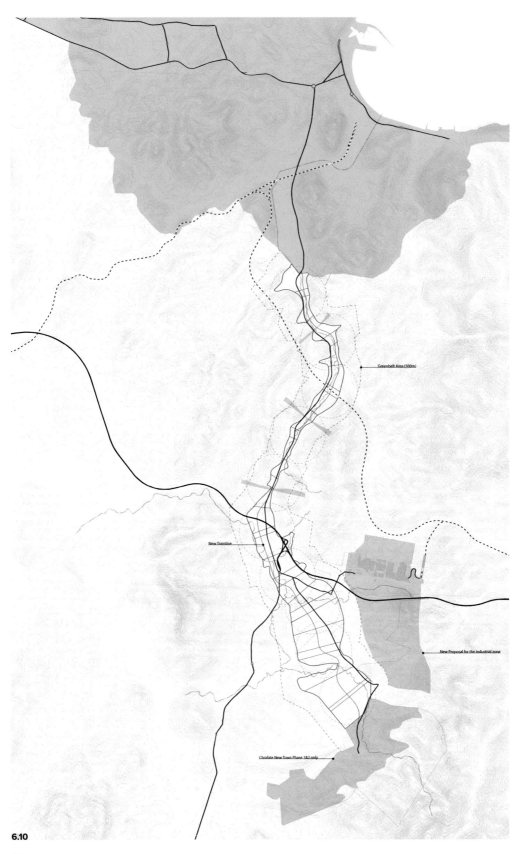

The Bartlett School of Architecture 2013

Greenbelt Area (500m)

New Tramline

New Proposal for the industrial zone

Chrafate New Town Phase 1&2 only

6.10

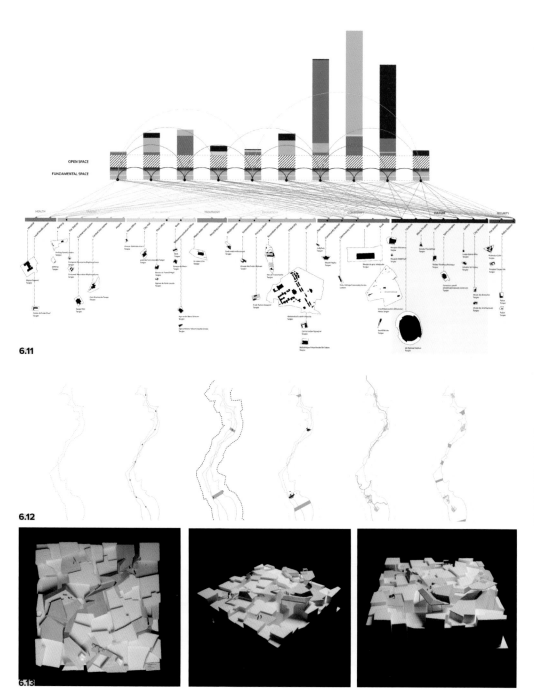

6.11

6.12

6.13

6.10 – 6.12 Young Joon Chung Uneven Tangier – Towards
Sustainable Urban Form. The Tangier Urban Agency currently
proposes a new urban boundary for the future expansion of
the city. This new limit is a bigger radius of the present centre,
without correspondence to topography. Selecting this form
of growth restricts access to public transportation and
sanitation. It will cause an increase in tariffs for poorer users,
resulting in areas lacking connection to the basic infrastructure
of the city. **6.10** Diagrammatic Plan **6.11** Typological study
6.12 Diagrammatic Plan **6.13 Nithita Fongtanakit** New Ground
- Public Spaces for Women. Conceptual models of the
proposed weaving co-operative located on the Medina rooftop.

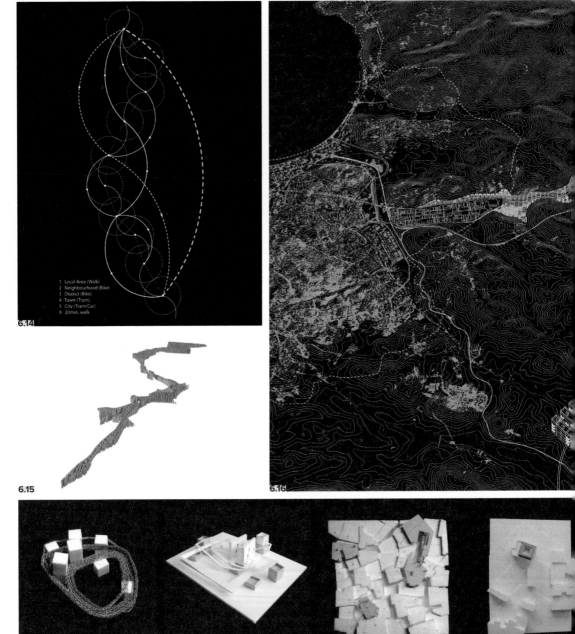

1 Local Area (Walk)
2 Neighbourhood (Bike)
3 District (Bike)
4 Town (Tram)
5 City (Tram/Car)
X 20min. walk

6.14

6.15

6.16

6.17

6.14 – 6.16 Young Joon Chung Uneven Tangier -Towards Sustainable Urban Form. **6.14** Rhythm diagram. **6.15** Urban massing. **6.16** Aerial view of the developed proposal. The project proposes to control growth of Tangier with new quality of life from mobilising infrastructure. It aims to expand Tangier linearly towards the new town of Chrafate by legally hijacking the basic infrastructure being installed to feed the new town. In the long term, this settlement will equalise with the satellite city giving more sustainability rather than isolation from Tangier. Growth is aimed not only in connecting two cities together but also suggests a new strategy of urban growth for the whole Tangier-Tetouan region. **6.17 Nithita Fongtanakit** New ground – Public Spaces for Women. Conceptual models of the proposed facilities. The project proposes a network of public facilities for supporting women in the current structure of the city, distributed in response to variations in population density. The interventions provide new spaces for gathering, job creation, education, discussion, and social interaction. The interventions are not centrally superimposed but respond to existing organisations and settings already identified within the city to provide facilities, funding, management and self-organisation. The network structure will form a co-operative to provide economic, labour and educational exchanges.

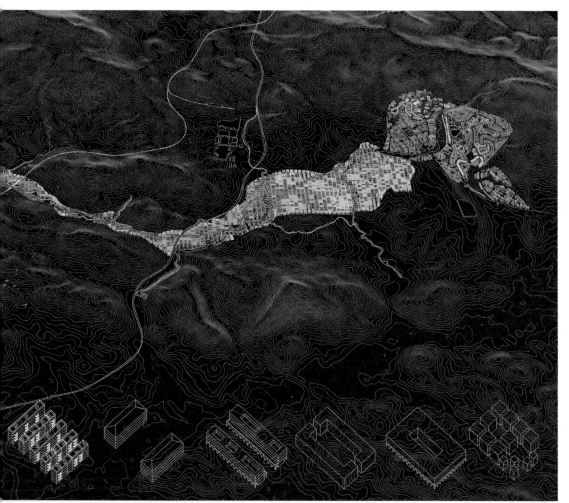

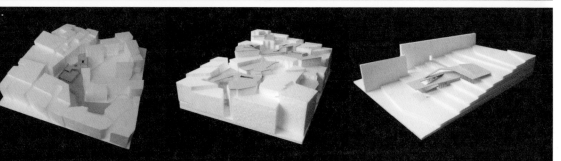

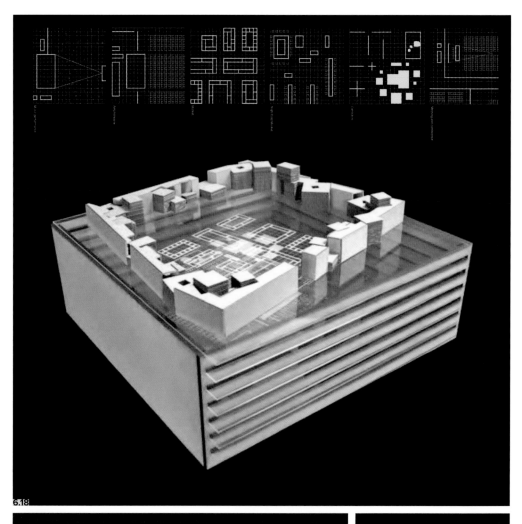

6.18

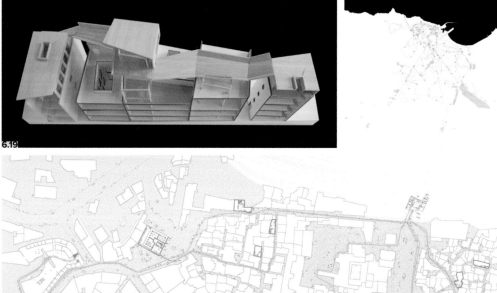

6.19

6.20

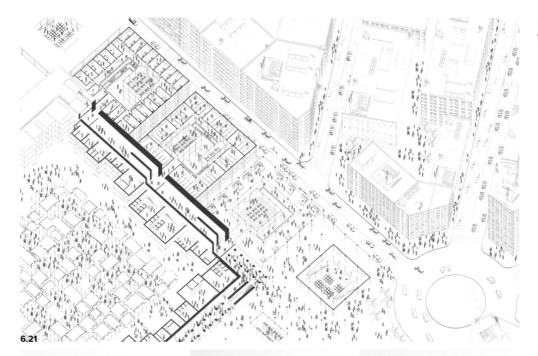

6.21

6.22

6.18 – 6.20 Nithita Fongtanakit New Ground - Public Spaces for Women. **6.19** Developed model of the proposed weaving co-operative located on the Medina rooftop and mapping of regional networks. **6.20** Ground plan of a network of facilities. **6.21 – 6.22 Hui Xu** The New Souk. **6.21** Axonometric cut-away of souk. **6.22** Visualisations looking out from the inside of the souk at inception, interim occupancy and maturation. The project attempts to use souk trading networks as a basis for developing the local economic and cultural environment. Each souk varies according to its specialised productions. It offers a meaningful way of cultural exchange besides Medinas in Morocco. Inherently souks are able to morph according to their surrounding typological demands. They are mutually informative and inter-relational. The New Souk's key functions are designed according to its 'living organism' nature so that it is able to stand strong against rejection process in an urbanised environment. The design strategy reconsiders and redesigns the key functions of the souk to fit the modern age.

6.23

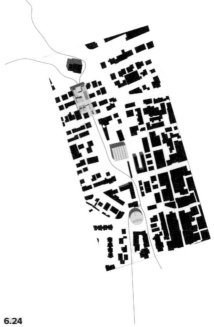

6.24

6.25

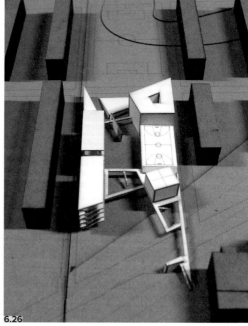

6.26

6.23 – 6.30 Hua Zua Education. **6.23 – 6.24** Mapping of Site 1: Bridging different neighbourhoods. **6.25 – 6.26** Map and model of Site 3: Engine of a new neighbourhood. **6.27 – 6.28** Map and model of Site 4: Link between industry and education. **6.29** Sectional model and conceptual plan of Site 4. **6.30** Tangier school typology study. The interaction between local neighbourhoods and educational activity is frequently neutral or even negative. In Tangier a dual problem exists of high levels of unemployment in highly educated sections of society combined with mass drop-out of population after primary school age. This project takes the model of 'the school of Athens' in treating education as an opportunity for communication and public space within the city. The participants' educational activities within or surrounding

the school are all the inhabitants rather than only students and teachers. Schools will interact with the neighbourhood where they are located, responding to the urban context of their location. The project works at three scales: 1. Tangier scale: the neighbourhoods in Tangier are mostly distributed fragmentally. The neighbourhood education facility would ideally be located in the centre of neighbourhoods to be easily accessed without crossing main roads. Reframing all the neighbourhoods by considering topographic, area, distance, and linear urban elements' cutting effect. Finding the initial ideal position of project through a series of calculations. 2. Neighbourhood scale: the project seeks to develop neighbourhoods by enhancing the public role of education facilities within them, in three stages. Firstly, by identifying 'connection centres',

6.27

6.28

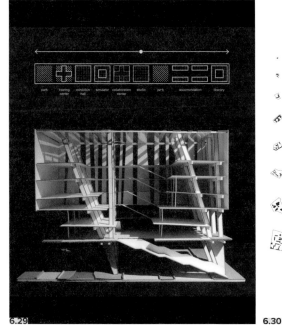

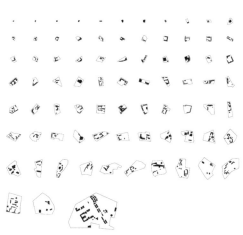

6.29

6.30

closer links are created within different groups and city infrastructures. Secondly, by formulating 'growth engines', the project creates strategies to encourage neighbourhood social and economic development in rapidly evolving sections of the city. Thirdly, by the creation of 'transformation catalysts', the project seeks to enhance less developed areas through educational activities. 3. Architecture scale: the basic structure of the school house could be abstracted into two pieces: the corridor and the classroom. The project dispatches these two parts and reinforces the public feature of the corridor aimed to create a common place for everyone in the neighbourhood.

6.31

6.32

6.33

6.31 Chung-Shing Huang Cruise Tourism – Visualisation of the New Port. Today, with the accomplishment of the Tanger Med Port, the cargo function of Tangier's old port has been replaced and the area is facing transformation. The proposal connects the existing touristic resources under the consideration of both the cruise tourist and the locals. It connects the cruise ship, existing embankment, ferry terminal, fishing port, and Kasbah on top of the Medina. It suggests a characteristic souk square surrounded by local shops, seafood restaurants, fishing market, and a port-side park. **6.32 – 6.33 Ching Wei Yang** N16. **6.32** Portion of regional map and development. **6.33** Visualisation of proposed housing. This project links villages along the Mediterranean highway (N16) to overcome local poverty and isolation in which the narcotics trade has flourished and to boost tourism. A series of location-specific interventions integrate farming, fishing, transportations, restaurants, and museums, reconciling local community needs, ecological characteristics and economic development. Seven strategies limit development, and connect the local community, tourism and the physical environment.

6.34

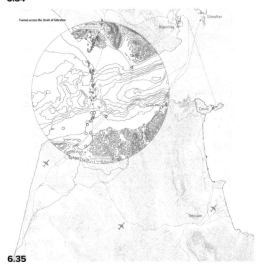

6.35

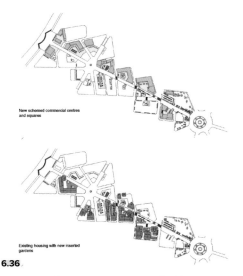

6.36

6.34 – 6.35 Shengwen Huang Connection. **6.34** Radial satellite village connected through new infrastructure link. **6.35** Gibraltar Strait rail link. The scheme connects the high speed rail terminals of national (Tanger Ville) and international (Gibraltar Strait Tunnel Terminal) establishing for the first time a complete Mediterranean and African network. The design project sits within the context of a wider investigation into the transformative impacts of international movement infrastructures. **6.36 Jiaoyang Fu** Coastal Connections. Diagrammatic plans. Tangier Bay is a leisure space for local people as well as an international holiday resort. At present, large numbers of hotels and holiday apartments are built densely along the beach and interrupt the direct relationship with the rest of the city. The project introduces a series of connections. The connections are axes of public space penetrating into the city as continuous physical and spatial paths. They function as expanded public space growing from the beach, attracting tourists to wander deeper into the city to make tourism benefit more areas.

6.37

6.38

6.37 – 6.38 Nina Vidic Connecting between. **6.37** Aerial view
of the proposal. **6.38** Local map of 'in-between' voids. Tangier
is as a border city known for its cultural, religious and social
diversity. Due to a weak state and no urban planning, there
is a lack of public facilities and poor infrastructure. Spaces in
between different neighbourhoods are left unused and not
maintained. The project utilises two repetitive modules to
organise the suburbs of Tangier. Besides creating visible
borders to contain the sprawl of single family houses the main
module also determines commercial streets and open squares
between different neighbourhoods and shifts the focus of the
community life from the hardly accessible and narrow streets
to the previously unused vacant space at the edges of the
neighbourhoods.

6.39

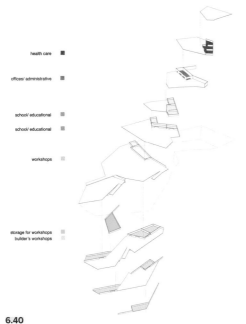

health care
offices/ administrative
school/ educational
school/ educational
workshops
storage for workshops
builder's workshops

6.40

6.41

6.39 – 6.41 Annick Meiers The void as incentive. **6.39** Regional function distribution map. **6.40** Exploded axonometric of platform functions. **6.41** Platform modelling. This proposal consists in different mechanisms of infill, as the implementation of a cluster of permanent, medium-scale, community sized social and civic structures, in combination with a rather nonessential structure, having the effect of a landmark, and public space, altogether called the 'platform'. These interventions are being developed based on an agreement between the state and the neighbourhoods' residents in order to ameliorate current living conditions in the 'non-regulated' areas. A series of temporary/pioneering interventions are part of the mechanisms of infill.

Tunis

7

Bio-UD

Claudia Pasquero, Marco Poletto

The dissolution of the dichotomy 'artifice vs. nature' opens new possibilities in the conception of the city from a non-anthropocentric perspective. Urban design can then be conceived as the breeding of relationships between industrial, agricultural, biological and social systems. Working on the emergent notion of 'agri-urbanity', this research cluster establishes a link between the instant/immaterial qualities of contemporary urbanism and the slow/material qualities that are the inextricable sign of the rural condition and its lifecycles.

Farming Energy in the Mediterranean: the Case of Tunisia

The studio begins with an examination of Tunis as an extended terrain for new practices of eco-social experimentation, on a micro social level and larger institutional scale. Four testbeds have been identified as examples of the territorial and conflictual dimension of contemporary urbanism: Bizerte, site of the largest reservoir of drinking water in Tunisia; the Tunis South Lake, site of a large and unregulated landfill; Sidi Bouzid, where most of Tunisian food is grown; and Tozeur, site of the future large scale DESERTEC solar energy farm.

An initial scan via indexical maps produced sets of operational fields, embryonic design contexts for the conception of urban prototypes, triggering and framing novel practices of farming energy and contributing to the growth of new self-sufficient city models. Each new urban prototype synthesises tectonic and material organisation from the introduction of specific biotechnologies into the test sites, connecting urban form to the creation of an independent and robust supply chain for food, energy, water and the transformation of waste.

The cluster adopts bio-inspired algorithmic design methods to draw terrains of negotiation across strategic and tactical forms of intervention; algorithmic coding enables the testing of design intentions across a fluid eco-social terrain,

generating a multiplicity of responses and effects across scales and regimes [from the molecular to the territorial]. Our research this year focussed on the advanced urban design application of four codes: Diffusion Limited Aggregation, deployed to test urban accretions in the Chott el Jerid Lake; Reaction Diffusion, to breed a bio-digestive landscape in the South Lake of Tunis; the Ants Foraging Behavior Model, to develop an edible landscape in Sidi Bouzid; and an Agent Based Ground Erosion Model, to evolve an artificial wetland terrain around Lake Ichkeul.

Working in small research teams, students identified partners that were invited to support a trans-disciplinary development of the design scenarios. Selected among scientists, sociologists, agronomists and engineers, key supporters were the leading industry consortium TuNur, building energy farms in Tunisia, the Department of Food, Environmental and Nutritional Sciences (DeFENS) – University of Milan and the UCL Department of Geography.

Pilot Cities

Each research team selected a pilot site in Tunisia. These were located in areas of conflict between the increasing need for resources of a growing city (Tunis) and an urbanising nation like Tunisia vs. the reduced capacity of the anthropised landscape to supply them. The case studies were treated as scenarios to design four new cities or models of urbanisation.

The Artificial Wetland City is located around Lake Ichkeul, one of the world's three most important bird sanctuaries. A protected UNESCO site, the lake's conditions have deteriorated due to increasing salinity and a sharp reduction in the numbers of migrating birds. Most of the missing fresh water is pumped 400km to feed Tunis and three other main cities. The artificial wetland model proposes to divert fresh water from the pipeline back to an artificial inhabited ground, where wetland habitat can be restored alongside agricultural, research and touristic activities. This new urban belt is organised around the lake to promote a new kind of active eco-urban conservation protocol.

The Activated Living Drosscape Project is located in South Lake of Tunis, now considered the most eutrophicated lagoon on the Tunisian coast. Its decay is the result of nutritious waste discharged by the jeans-washing factories, food-producing industries, and others since the 1970s. The project proposes a new model of bio-technological landscape devoted to the bio-digestion of industrial and residential waste by means of algal microorganisms; here, urban "green" becomes a biological machine for transformation whereby nutrients and raw material are produced right in the heart of the city.

The Edible Landscape augments the city of Sidi Bouzid, located in central Tunisia, one of the main agricultural hubs of the country. Climate change, the rising price of food and reliance on global imports of wheat are placing great pressures on farmers to produce. Edible Landscape deploys lightweight and low-tech farming kits to create a new self-organising infrastructure able to augment productivity and introduce new food streams; the infrastructure is controlled by a robust and adaptive urban code that provides constant reconfiguration in response to changing environmental stimuli, offering microclimatic control, bio-energy production and new trading opportunities.

The Nomadic Renewable Energy Networks is a new power-exporting city located in the Chott el Jerid lake near Tozeur. The area is site for the development of a large-scale solar concentrator plant, part of the TuNur initiative. The project proposes to substitute the centralised plant with a diffuse form of renewable energy harvesting, based on a network of nomadic hubs powered by multiple forms energy available in the lake, including solar, wind, geothermal and biological. The robust

infrastructure will host 30,000 inhabitants including local Bedouins, traditional inhabitants of these extreme environments.

Special thanks to: Peter Bishop, Lucy Bullivant, Marcos Cruz, Stephen Gage, Ruairi Glynn, Evan Greenberg, George Jeronimidis, Enriqueta Llabres, Frédéric Migayrou, Andrew Porter, Alfredo Ramirez, Eduardo Rico, Peg Rawes, Jose Sanchez, Eva Sopeoglou and Elia Zenghelis.

Students
Yi (Eva) Ge, Artemis Karaiskou, Antonios Lalos, Shi Min Pong, Anna Sideri, Ruowei Song, Li (Vincent) Wang, Zi (Anna) Wang, Ting (Wendi) Wen, Jing (Jill) Zhang, Luoyao Zhu

Project teams
Sidi Bouzid Shi Min Pong, Ruowei Song, Ting (Wendi) Wen
Lake Ichkeul Yi (Eva) Ge, Zi (Anna) Wang, Luoyao Zhu
South Lake Tunis Li (Vincent) Wang, Jing (Jill) Zhang
Chott el Jerid Artemis Karaiskou, Antonios Lalos, Anna Sideri

http://udtunis.wix.com/biourb

Electricity Demand
EU & MENA Countries

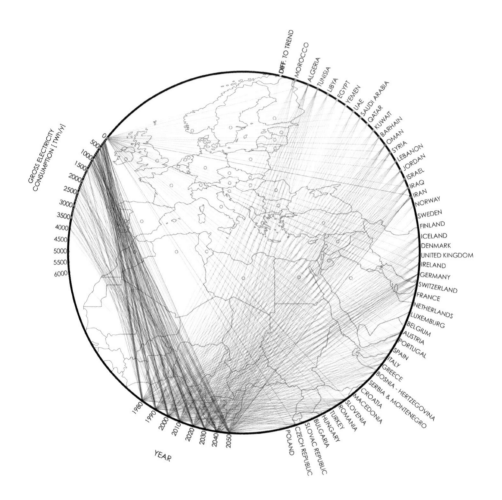

7.1

7.1 Antonios Lalos The Gross Consumption of Energy in the EUMENA countries from 1980 to 2050 [predicted]. Since most of the countries are moving from being creditors to becoming debtors new resources have to be found and moved across the region. The Mediterranean Solar Plan is an eco-political project that has been initiated with the ambition to develop a renewable energy network spanning Europe, north Africa and the Middle East to collect energy in the energy rich regions of the Sahara and redistribute to energy indebted countries such as Germany. Tunisia among others has transformed into a new potential ground for production and has, as a consequence, become a disputed terrain for a new form of industrial development and energetic colonialism. **7.2 Antonios Lalos** The ground morphology of

Tunisia - processed satellite map. **7.3 – 7.5 Chott el Jerid** Territories. The Chott el Jerid lake, near Tozeur. **7.3** Satellite view. 7.4 An artificial pond of salty brine. **7.5** A sample of the superficial crust of the lake containing biologically active layers of cianobacteria. **7.6 – 7.8 South Lake Tunis** Territories. South Lake, Tunis. **7.6** Natural wetland in the abandoned old port of Tunis **7.7** Agro-industrial terrain at the edge of the Lake, only 1km from the centre of Tunis. **7.8** Samples of algal organisms collected in the lake; such biologic machines have incredible photosynthetic abilities.

7.2

7.3

7.4

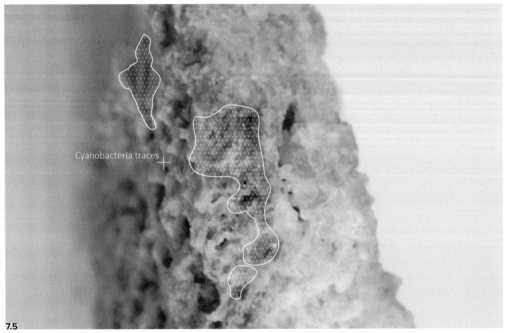

Cyanobacteria traces

7.5

7.6

7.7

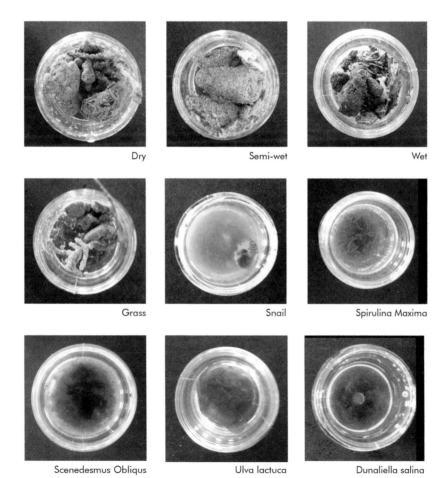

| Dry | Semi-wet | Wet |

| Grass | Snail | Spirulina Maxima |

| Scenedesmus Obliqus | Ulva lactuca | Dunaliella salina |

7.8

7.9 – 7.11 Lake Ichkeul Territories. Lake Ichkeul, Bizerte, in the
north of Tunisia **7.9** A dry and dying wetland now turned into
grazing terrain for local cattle. **7.10** One of the four major dams
collecting water form the Ichkeul basin to feed the four main
cities of Tunisia. **7.11** The pipeline travelling 400km from north
to south Tunisia feeding drinking water to large portions of the
urban population. **7.12 – 7.14 Sidi Bouzid** Territories. Sidi
Bouzid, central Tunisia **7.12** Satellite view of the town and
the surrounding agricultural land, one of the biggest food
producing hub in the country. **7.13** View of one of the local
Wadi, dried rivers now used mainly as recreational spaces.
7.14 Gatrana, a pioneering project in Sidi Bouzid, farming
algae for human consumption and food supplement, result
of an Anglo-Tunisian joint venture.

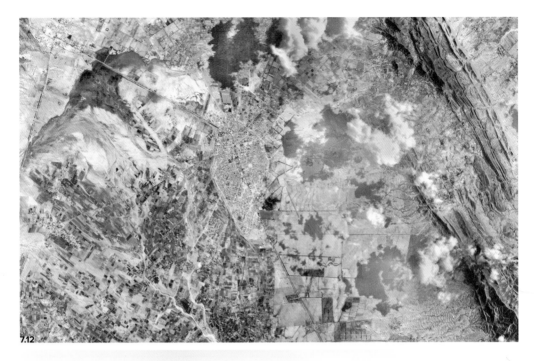

7.12

7.13

ORGANIC DIY ALGAE FARM

ALG

"SPIRULINA WILL BE THE
NEXT BIG THING IN THE FOOD
INDUSTRY... IT IS GOING TO
THE MICRO-ORGANISM WITH
A BIG IMPACT FOR THE FUTURE"
Nizar Chouchene, Senior Engineer at Bio Gatrana

// NETWORK
Organic DIY Algae Cultivation

// ACTORS + AGENTS
Spirulina Algae
French visionaries and investors
Engineer and technicians
Laboratory

7.14

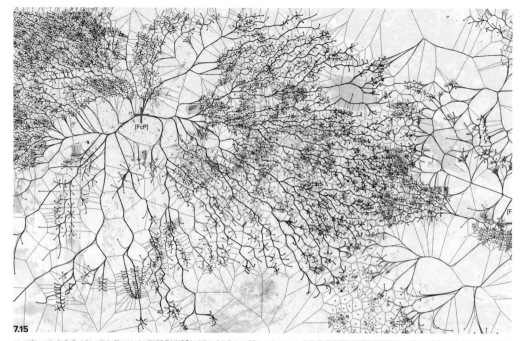

7.15

7.16

7.15 – 7.17 Sidi Bouzid Operational Fields **7.15** Projective Food Networks. The field is computed by tracing minimal paths between food producing plots and existing distribution markets. As the production fluctuates so does the network which adapts by adjusting the position or dimension of the paths. The concept of a nomadic market emerged from the iterative application of this machinic device. **7.16** Water Flow Patterns and Collection Points. The algorithmic map reads topographic data and rain patterns to compute patterns of distribution and collection of rain water across the agricultural territory creating a potential field of intensified cultivation as well as an indication of potential erosion and desertification. **7.17** Multi-layered Model of Operational Territories. The model materialises a projective terrain for the breeding of a new edible landscape; each layer is read as a stimulus for action/reaction and for the computation of a new agricultural protocol.

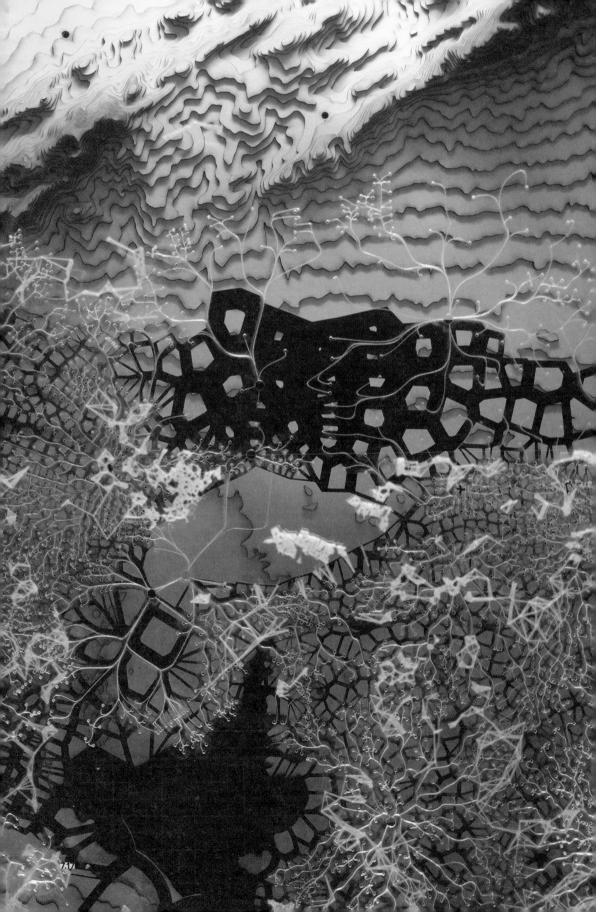

7.18

7.19

7.18 – 7.19 Lake Ichkeul Operational Fields **7.18** Rain Water Collection Network. Computed in relationship to topography and existing agricultural plot tessellation **7.19** Projective Map for a New Artificial Wetland Landscape. Each plot is computed in relationship to slope, wetness and existing agricultural resolution; the size of the network branches is proportional to slope, speed and surface roughness. **7.20 South Lake Tunis** Operational Fields. Algae Farming Potential Terrain. The virtual plots are computed in relationship to existing bathymetry, eutrophication levels and resolution of typical urban plots in the surrounding areas. **7.21 – 7.22 Chott el Jerid Lake** Operational Fields **7.21** Simulation of emergent bio-energy production centres computed with an agent based model of diffusion limited aggregation, related to existing sources of

cianobacteria around the salty ponds. **7.22** Material aggregation patterns at the edge of the lake, evidencing the transition between sandy dynamic dunes, salty semi-liquid terrain and crystallised salt-gypsum ground.

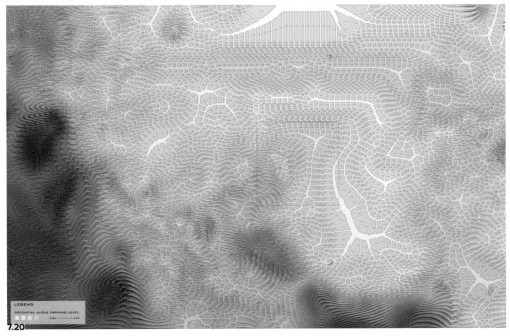

LEGEND
POTENTIAL ALGAE FARMING LEVEL

7.20

7.21

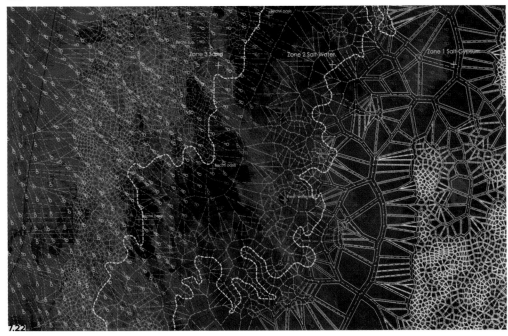

Zone 3 Sand   Zone 2 Salt-Water   Zone 1 Salt-Gypsum

7.22

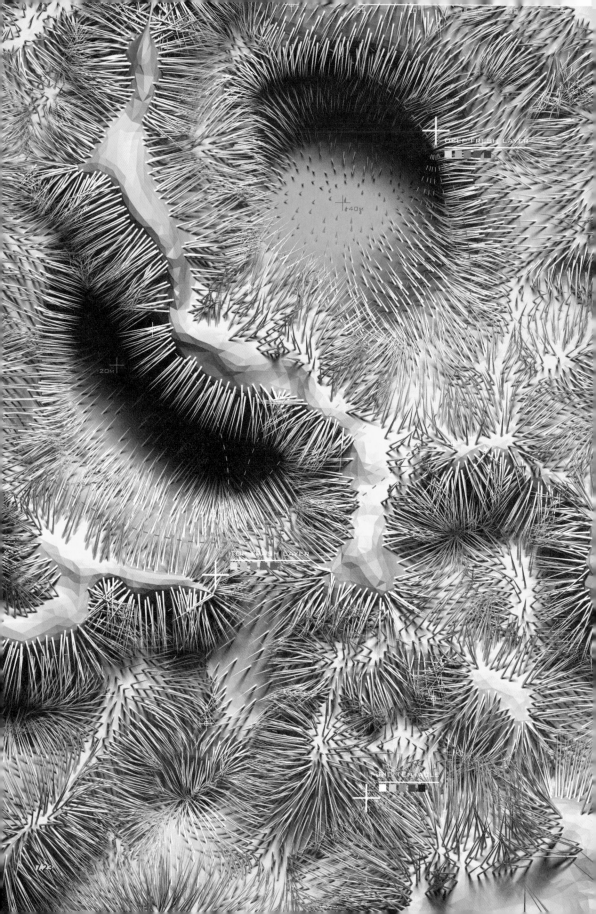

7.24

7.25

7.26

7.27

7.23 – 7.24 South Lake Tunis Prototypes – Living Activated Drosscape **7.23** Top view of the bio-digesting landscape, with the super-grass tendrils. Each tendril combines an engineered soft substratum with a layer of active biofilm able to filter polluted water and digest organic and metallic particles. **7.24** The drosscape panorama at the edge of the existing village on the south shore of the lake. **7.25 – 7.27 Sidi Bouzid** Prototypes – Edible Landscape Kit Panoramic Views **7.25** Augmented grazing within the new algae farming landscape. Geolocated flying hydropods transport hydrogen gas across the city following energy demand levels on the ground. **7.26** The solar powered Wadi Cloud floats above the landscape regulating the microclimate below and intensifying traditional farming through due collection and percolation.

7.27 The Nomadic Market structure sediments over busiest transport nodes providing solar shading and promoting local trading of new farming products.

7.28

7.29

7.30

7.31

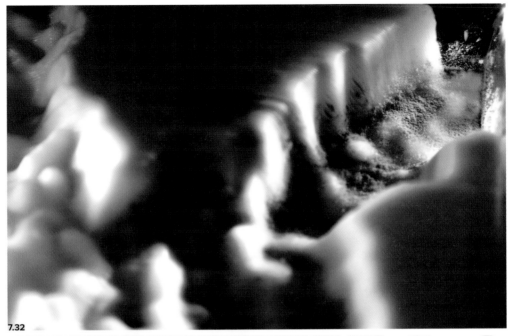

7.32

7.33

7.28 Ichkeul Lake Prototypes – Infrastrcutural Wetland Bird's-eye view of artificial wetland prototype town. The village emerges in the belt of land between the Ichkeul dam piping line and its main tributary. A system of pipes is hacking the main infrastructure diverting water towards the tributary through an artificially articulated ground surface that provides areas of differentiated wetness. **7.29 – 7.33 Chott el Jerid Lake** Prototypes **7.29** View of the Bedouin Powerhouse from the surrounding camp. The prototype provides an infrastructure for the farming of bacteria for bio-energy production. **7.30** The Water Hub Mountain converts a fossil water well into a centre for the production of renewable energy via hydrolysis and salt by evaporation and sedimentation. **7.31** The Dune Lab hosts a research centre for bacteric experimentation while proposing a new construction method to consolidate sediment sand into bio-stone dunes. **7.32** Bedouine Powerhouse sample: 3D printed model with inoculated cianobacterial cultures. **7.33** Water hub prototype: electrolytic cells within vacum formed plexy skin.

7.34

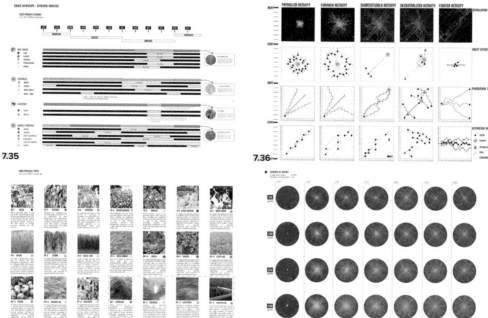

7.35

7.36

7.37

7.38

7.34 – 7.38 Sidi Bouzid Team Simulated Cities **7.34** Top view of simulated edible landscape with emergent production clusters, transport and trading paths. **7.35** Time chart for introduction of novel agricultural system. **7.36** Agent-based simulation parameters and agent behaviours. **7.37** Local agricultural biodiversity. **7.38** Parametric studies of agents' behaviour in relationship to specific ground conditions and cultivation time chart. **7.39 – 7.41 Chott el Jerid Lake** Simulated Cities **7.39** Bird's-eye view of the simulated city from the edge of the lake. **7.40** Diagram illustrating the urban code with key flows of matter, information and energy across and among the prototypes. **7.41** Parametric Studies of Diffusion Limited Aggregation. The key parameters include seeds location, ground and wind conditions as well as aggregation distances

in relationship to typical Bedouin camp. **7.42 – 7.43 South Lake Tunis** Simluated Cities **7.42** Plan of simulated scenario of drosscape and biotechnological city based on reaction diffusion algorithm. **7.43** Bird's-eye view of drosscape from the lake side showing bio-active super-grass waste digesting cavities, infrastructures and inhabited islands. The islands are built by extending the local port technology into reconfigurable container buildings.

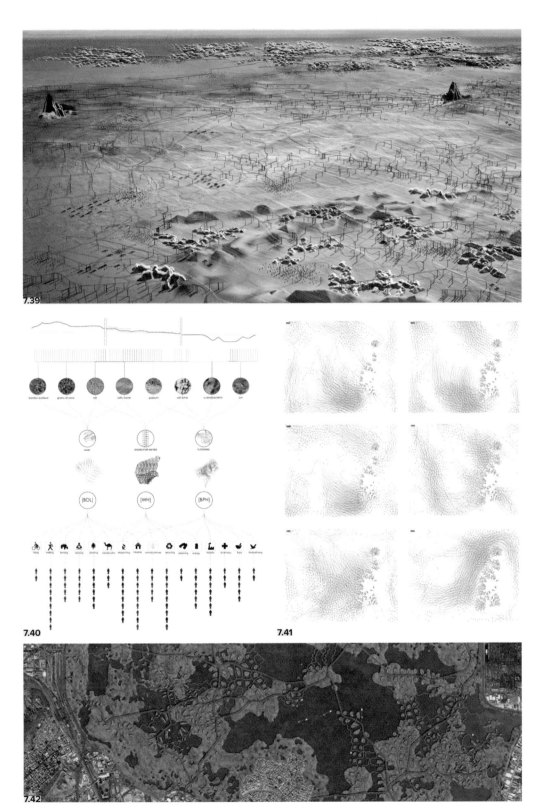

7.39

7.40

7.41

7.42

7.43

Group photo of the Algiers Cluster on their field trip to Morocco in front of the Hassan II Mosque in Casablanca

Marseille field trip

fletcher priest architects
trust

Bartlett Lectures

The **Bartlett International Lecture Series** features speakers from across the world. Lectures in the series are open to the public and free to attend.

This year's speakers included:

Rob Adams
Ben Addy
Yannis Aesopos
Ben van Berkel
Aaron Betsky
Iain Borden
Benjamin Bratton
Mario Carpo
Peter Cook
Nat Chard
Raffaello D'Andrea
Graham Harman
Jonathan Hill
Luca Galofaro
Giuseppe Longo
Kengo Kuma
Winy Maas
Gurjit Singh Matharoo
Achim Menges
Nicholas de Monchaux
Gianni Pettena
Dominique Perrault
Wolfgang Rieder
Joseph Rykwert
Philippe Rahm
Casey Reas
Jenny E Sabin
Bob Sheil
Kristina Schinegger and Stefan Rutzinger
Tezuka Takaharu
Timothy Wray and Andrew Higgott

The Bartlett International Lecture Series is generously sponsored by the Fletcher Priest Trust.

A new range of smaller lecture series' attracted over 50 speakers to our Royal Ear Hospital building.

Bartlett Nexus
Maj Plemenitas, Gennaro Senatore, Ezio Blasetti, Paul Nicholls, Tobias Klein, Madhav Kidao, Jack Munro, Michail Desyllas, Gregory Epps, Kate Davies, Slub, Catrina Stewart, Tom Betts, Matt Johnson, Ollie Palmer, Manja van de Worp, Marcus Wendt and Vera-Maria Glahn, Memo Akten, Mollie Claypool, Ines Dantas, Niccolo Casas, Martin Dittus, Cohen Van Balen, Vlad Tenu, Gilles Retsin, Ryan Mehanna, Tom Smith

Effective Knowledge
Emilie Hergott, Nicolas Bredeche, Justin Dirrenberger, Andrew Witt, Lucia Mondardini, Niccolo Baldasssini

Material Matters
Daniel Bosa, Enrico Dini, Matt Wade, Ollie Palmer

Bartlett lectures can be viewed at **vimeo.com/bartlettarchucl**

Staff

Professor Frédéric Migayrou
Bartlett Professor of
Architecture, Chair
B-Pro Director

Dr Marcos Cruz
Reader in Architecture
Director of School

Professors

Professor Peter Bishop
Professor of Urban Design

Professor Iain Borden
Professor of Architecture
& Urban Culture
Vice Dean of Communications
Director of History & Theory

Professor Adrian Forty
Professor of Architectural
History
MA Architectural History
Programme Director

Professor Colin Fournier
Professor of Urban Design

Professor Murray Fraser
Professor of Architecture
& Global Culture
Vice Dean of Research

Professor Stephen Gage
Professor of Innovative
Technology

Professor Christine Hawley
Professor of Architectural
Studies
Director of Design

Professor Jonathan Hill
Professor of Architecture
& Visual Theory
MPhil/PhD by Design
Programme Director

Professor CJ Lim
Professor of Architecture
& Cultural Design
Vice Dean of International
Affairs

Professor Jane Rendell
Professor of Architecture & Art
Vice Dean of Research

Professor Bob Sheil
Professor of Architecture and
Design through Production
Director of Technology and
Computing

Academic Staff

Laura Allen
Senior Lecturer
BSc Architecture Programme
Director

Alisa Andrasek
Lecturer in Advanced
Architectural Computation
MArch GAD Programme
Leader

Julia Backhaus
MArch Architecture
Programme Director

Dr Jan Birksted
Principal Research Associate
Coordinator Year 3 History &
Theory

Matthew Butcher
Lecturer in Architecture and
Performance
Coordinator of Pedagogic
Affairs

Dr Ben Campkin
Lecturer in History & Theory
Director of Urban Lab

Dr Marjan Colletti
Senior Lecturer
Acting MArch Architecture
Programme Director

Ruairi Glynn
Lecturer in Interactive
Architecture

Dr Penelope Haralambidou
Lecturer in Architecture
Coordinator of MPhil / PhD by
Design

Dirk Krolikowski
Lecturer in Innovative
Technology & Design Practice
Associate Coordinator of Year
4 Design Realisation

Dr Adrian Lahoud
Reader in Urban Design
MArch UD Programme Leader

Dr Yeoryia Manolopoulou
Senior Lecturer
Director of Architectural
Research

James O'Leary
Lecturer in Innovative
Technology & Design Practice
Coordinator of Year 4 Design
Realisation

Dr Barbara Penner
Senior Lecturer
BSc Architectural Studies
Programme Director
MPhil/PhD History & Theory
Programme Director

Frosso Pimenides
Senior Lecturer
BSc Architecture Year 1
Director

Andrew Porter
B-Pro Deputy Director

Dr Peg Rawes
Senior Lecturer
Associate Director of
Architectural Research

Dr Tania Sengupta
Lecturer in Architectural
History & Theory
Coordinator of Year 2 / Year 4
History & Theory

Mark Smout
Senior Lecturer
Acting Director of Technology
and Computing

Susan Ware
Sub-Dean and Faculty Tutor
Director of Professional
Studies
Part 3 Programme Director

Patrick Weber
Lecturer
BSc Architecture Year 1
Director

Research Fellows & Visiting Professors

Niall McLaughlin
Visiting Professor

Dr Hilary Powell
Research Fellow

Professional Services

**Academic Services
Administration**
Rachael Burnett
Michelle Bush
Emer Girling
Tom Mole

Research
Luis Rego

Communications and Website
Laura Cherry
Jean Garrett
Michelle Lukins

Finance and HR
Sarah Clegg
Stoll Michael
Sheetal Saujani

Professional Studies
Kim Macneill
Indigo Rohrer
Naz Siddique

Facilities
Graham Kennett
John Riley
Dave Yates

B-Made
Abi Abdolwahabi
Martin Avery
Sarat Babu
Richard Beckett
Matt Bowles
Bim Burton
Inigo Dodd
Justin Goodyer
Richard Grimes
Edgardo de Lara
Robert Randall
Paul Smoothy
Emmanuel Vercruysse
Martin Watmough

MArch UD Staff

Professor Frédéric Migayrou
B-Pro Director

Andrew Porter
B-Pro Deputy Director

Adrian Lahoud
Programme Leader

Graciela Moreno
Programme Coordination
Tutor

Research Cluster Tutors

Algiers
Beth Hughes
DaeWha Kang

Athens
Yannis Aesopos
Ross Exo Adams

Beirut
Aristide Antonas
Sam Jacoby

Marseille
Platon Issaias
Camila Sotomayor

Messina & Reggio Calabria
Luca Galafaro
Davide Sacconi

Tangiers
Jonathan Kendall
Peter Besley
Hannah Corlett

Tunis
Claudia Pasquero
Marco Poletto

History & Theory Tutors

Ross Exo Adams
Mollie Claypool
Sam Jacoby
Godofredo Pereira
Lorenzo Pezzani

External Examiners

Professor Bart Lootsma
Eric Parry RA
Professor Lola Sheppard
Professor Tom Verebes

Critics and Consultants

Isabel Allen
Medine Altiok
Ottavio Amaro
Morad Ameziane
Andreas Angelidakis
Aristide Antonas
Abigail Ashton
Pier Vittorio Aureli
Petros Babasikas
Andrea Bagnato
Peter Bishop
Harris Biskos
Abdellatif Brini
Lucy Bullivant
Matthew Butcher
Hussam Chakouf
Yasmina El Chami
Christopher Choa
Dimitris Christopoulos
Marcos Cruz
Brian Dale
Eddy Declerc
Orsalia Dimitrou
Panos Dragonas
Tarsha Finney
William Firebrace
Maria Giudici
Ruairi Glynn
Sakiko Goto
Evan Greenberg
Aref Hassani
Jonathan Hill
Rachid Houari
Alberto Iacovoni
Mohamed Jallal
George Jeronimidis
Dimitra Katsota
Hicham Kersit
Andreas Kourkoulas
El Moumni Lahbib
Marina Lathouri
Enriqueta Llabres
Kieran Long
Fadi Mansour
Gabriele Mastrigli
Johnny Ojeil
John Palmesino
Daniel Fernandez Pascual

Carlos Perez Marin
Angelo Plessas
Alfredo Ramirez
Peg Rawes
Jane Rendell
Charles Rice
Eduardo Rico
Robert Saliba
Hassan Salmi M'Rabet
Jose Sanchez
Ivonne Santoyo Orozco
Patrick Schumacher
Francesco Sebregondi
Maha Shuayb
Eva Sopeoglou
Douglas Spencer
Naiara Vegara
Yuwei Wang
Eyal Weisman
Peter Wynne Rees
Nikos Xydakis
Yiorgis Yerolymbos
Thanos Zartaloudis
Elia Zenghelis

bartlett.ucl.ac.uk/architecture

Publisher
Bartlett School of Architecture, UCL

Editors
Frédéric Migayrou, Andrew Porter

Graphic Design
Patrick Morrissey, Unlimited
weareunlimited.co.uk

Editorial Coordination
Michelle Lukins, Laura Cherry

ISBN 978-0-9572355-7-1

For more information on all the programmes and
modules at The Bartlett Faculty of the Built
Environment, UCL, visit bartlett.ucl.ac.uk

The Bartlett School of Architecture, UCL
Wates House
Gordon Street
London WC1H 0QB
T. +44 (0)20 7679 7504
F. +44 (0)20 7679 4831
architecture@ucl.ac.uk

Bartlett Prospective